TOP DOGS

TOP DOGS

A celebration of great Australian working dogs

Angela Goode

ABC
Books

Introduction

When I made the innocent observation 25 years ago that working dogs could teach us humans a thing or two, I never anticipated the stardom they would enjoy. Working dogs now surely have reached the heights of fame with this magnificent book of photographs and stories contributed by ABC local and regional radio listeners. Portrayed as they work, sleep and play, their huge personalities leap off the page. It is a truly astonishing record of life as it is lived on farms, through the eyes of working dogs.

It was a foggy winter morning in 1989 when I saw two kelpies bounding through mud behind an ag bike to go mustering. As I watched them in my rear-vision mirror, their infectious enthusiasm made me smile. Human workers at the time were threatening to strike for more pay and fewer hours. Yet here were workers for whom having a job was reward enough. It was a mighty contrast with the grizzling coming from the car radio that morning. The idea of praising the joyous workaholism of working dogs was born that day as I drove to Adelaide to deliver my weekly chat for the ABC's *Country Hour*. I spoke of the work ethic of dogs – and it unleashed something quite extraordinary. Farm people everywhere picked up pens to tell stories of their dogs' heroism and hard work, and of a bond so close between human and dog that they could read each other's minds. Admiration and devotion flowed from the pages. They told of workmates that never went on strike, never complained about mud, dust, heat, frost, prickles or long hours. More than 300 of these stories, from more than 3,000 received, were published in the *Great Working Dog* series of books, loved and cherished far and wide.

So, 25 years later, we celebrate the talents of working dogs with these remarkable photographs shot on the dogs' own turf. These images take you to places far from the cities, way off the bitumen, to where cattle, sheep and goats graze. Rural people from all

over Australia have revealed, through their dogs, authentic insights into the lives they lead and the work they do producing food and fibre. Like their dogs, they can't go on strike: two-legged versions of their four-legged workaholics!

More than a thousand images bursting with energy, character and exuberance made the judging of the best hundred images to be included in this book a hugely difficult task. So, may I suggest a nationwide round of applause for the photographers of regional Australia! Many images took my breath away: such sharp and astonishing action, such athleticism and character, and so many shots revealing layers of the story without a need for words. Many of their captions though are as poignant as a short story. I congratulate every one of these talented and instinctive photographers.

I am delighted that so many images perfectly complement the stories included in this book. These were chosen as the very best of those published in *Great Australian Working Dog Stories* and they are still as vibrant and as genuine as the day they were first written. They tell of dogs making long trips home, working solo out bush, saving lives, or just being great and empathetic companions. To those who shared their stories with me over the years, I thank you.

I defy you not to smile as you turn the pages of this book. As well as the bond between dog and human, there's trust, a crazy sense of fun, and plenty of canine wisdom in knowing eyes. This collection of images and stories will touch you as surely as a dog dozing at the end of a tough working day, its head resting on your arm.

Angela Goode, 2014

Age shall not weary the ways of a kelpie! Bill is seventeen and stills feels more comfortable on the back of a ute than anywhere else. **Sally Harding, Albury, NSW**

My dog Els

Rob Williams Albury, NSW

The strength, fitness, flexibility and agility of the working farm dog never cease to amaze me. I took this photo of my border collie Cameo as she changed direction mid-stride while working the sheep. On the property there isn't a sheep she can't control: she can outrun, outwit and move the most difficult sheep. Yet when there are ewes with lambs to move, she's so gentle and calm, it's Cameo we choose every time. She'll still work the ewe to where we need her to be, but she seems to pass a telepathic message to the ewe that she will in no way harm her lamb. We bred from her once and she was a wonderful mother to her pups, and I'm sure it's this extra special maternal instinct that has remained with her and made her the perfect all round sheepdog.
**Janice De Gennaro,
Windsor, SA**

I won her in a pub at Blackall. She was mostly blue cattle dog plus something else. So that's what I called her—Els.

She was easy enough to train, but most of the time she'd do something else first. Being a patient sort of bloke, this didn't worry me too much.

I had two other dogs who were good workers and Els soon copied them. But she always included some other job as an extra. She believed she was a star. As it turned out, she was.

I got a job moving a small mob of cattle, all a bit rough, from Nardoo way, north to Cloncurry, about 1,200 kilometres away. This was back in the fifties. The country was bloody dry and hot, and because I was broke, I took on this job alone.

There were just three dogs, three horses and me – and any quids at the end were all mine! I wasn't worried about putting condition on the cattle. I was pushing them fast and my team and I really worked.

About two days run from the 'Curry, my horse Sampson caught his foot in a hole and fell with me pinned beneath him. He was trapped and I was too. I found out later that my leg was busted in two places and I was concussed.

I came round some time later with Sampson thrashing wildly every so often, and two dogs sitting in some shade, but no bloody Els. She'd run off. I thought I'd had it.

Now this is what Els did. She ran all right—in a straight line to the only two blokes within 80 kilometres. How she knew, I'll never know.

These blokes were fencing. They told me that this sweaty looking, tired dog came up, barking at them, and pulling at the pants of the bloke with the wire. He thought she was mad and hit her, but she kept circling, barking and running off. She did this four or five times.

In the bush, the real blokes get a feeling about things. I can't explain it. These blokes, God bless them, got that feeling. They climbed into their ute and followed her. It was only about ten kilometres but she led them straight back to me and I suppose that's the end of the story.

Els should have looked after the cattle. She could have had a laze in the shade, but that dear, wonderful bitch did something.

Grinning from ear to ear

Val Pate Renmark, SA

When we were first married, my husband owned a nondescript red kelpie called Sailor. He was a constant companion as well as a workmate on our partly developed property at Mingenew in WA, some miles from the nearest neighbour.

In mid-January one year, we were doing some contract harvesting about five miles from our home for a neighbour. Just after lunch during the hottest part of the day, we took a load of grain into the local siding, leaving Sailor with the tractor and header. We considered it would be kinder and cooler than taking him in the hot truck with us.

On our return Sailor was missing. We thought he had taken umbrage at being left and had returned home. When we discovered he wasn't at home, we tracked his paw prints for about eight miles along the dirt road heading north into town, until nightfall prevented us going further.

Next morning we headed into town 22 miles away and asked around if anyone had seen him. No luck. We proceeded on to visit my parents, nineteen miles north of town, to be greeted by my furious father and a very contented Sailor grinning from ear to ear.

The night before, he had locked, so he thought, his bitch in the shearing shed in solitary confinement for the duration of her heat—only to be greeted in the morning by two happy dogs lying peacefully side by side.

Sailor had been with us three weeks earlier when we all had Christmas with my parents. He had not seen his young lady since, but had been quite prepared to walk 48 miles in the heat, somehow knowing the timing would be right. And to think we had been feeling sorry for him.

Joyce is the lady of the station and now does what she pleases. She is a wonderfully loyal friend, often sitting next to me on the front seat of the ute while the other workers are tied up on the back. Now she is semi-retired, Joyce picks and chooses her work days. In the morning, she enjoys walking down the road, followed by a cup of tea on the veranda. **Tom Ellis, Mt Gambier, SA**

City slicker

Charlie Bryce Yankalilla, SA

As a boy, I spent most of my spare time wandering the different places in the bush where we lived. I walked the hills of the Barossa, explored the wide flat country of Keith and trekked through the sandhills near Robe. Always by my side was my mate, Spike.

His mother was a stray who was caught killing sheep. She was about to be shot when it was noticed she was heavily pregnant. We let her have the pups and Spike was the one I chose to keep. He wasn't very handsome but I didn't care. He made up for his lack of looks by quickly learning everything I taught him. He would sit until I told him to move, sometimes for half an hour. He would bark, fetch balls, jump, come, go and I think he even tried to speak. Anyway, we were great mates. Sometimes when it was very cold, I'd even sneak him inside and let him sleep on my bed. Mum never found out because he had learned to tiptoe silently.

Eventually, I went off to ag college. Dad had died so Mum moved to the city. She looked after him for me and in return he gave her company and barked at strangers.

When I finished my three-year course, I went off to be a jackeroo in station country down south. They were running 20,000 merinos and I was one of twelve jackeroos. Every bloke had to have a dog. Some of the big shots had two. The dog you had, how smart and good-looking it was, in a way defined your manhood.

I had a problem. With Mum widowed and not much money to go around among the eight of us, there was no way I could get a fancy sheepdog for myself. Spike was all I had. He was ten years old and had never seen sheep because we only had cattle or crops on the places where Dad had worked. He appeared to have a bit of working dog in him and was a bloody good fighter, so he was good enough for me. I knew that if anyone laughed at his funny-shaped body or tatty ears, I could set him onto his dog. There's no greater crime in the bush than criticising a bloke's dog. You can say his wife or girlfriend's ugly but you can't laugh at his dog.

So I roll up with my old mate sitting on the front seat beside me in my ute. He would have been offended if I had put him in the back. He peered down his scarred old nose at all the mutts that came out from under the jackeroos' quarters to bark at us. When he alighted, he regally peed on the wheel of my ute, surveyed the milling throng and trotted stiffly, with his head in the air and his hackles bristling slightly, with me to my room. He slept on my bed and accepted his change of address without any fuss.

Next morning, we assembled by the quarters to be briefed and get our day's jobs from the manager. Most of the time we couldn't hear him because, if you can imagine twelve blokes all with at least one dog, and the boss with his dog, it was one big dogfight.

The boss's dog was the worst. It seemed to know he was the top dog, so to speak. He went around picking on all the other dogs, giving them a nip or a push in a sneaky, thuggish sort of way. As underlings and me being new to the place, we couldn't do anything much about it. When one dog did snarl in retaliation, the boss's kelpie hurled himself at him and fought until the other was a bloody mess.

Our boss pretended not to notice. He just droned on as though nothing was happening—even though the rolling, screaming

Little Boxie's mother performed every day for the crowds at Luke Thomas's stock show at the Australian Stockman's Hall of Fame in Longreach. After a brief encounter with an amorous working Kelpie from Goulburn, she whelped under the worker's cottage around which the show is performed. Luke offered Nic a pup and she came to live at Rio Station, 15 kilometres southwest of Longreach. After a day's sheep work in the yards it started to rain, and the ewes had to be taken down and out the laneway, about five kilometres. To get Boxie used to all conditions, Nic took her with him on the bike. As a winter night's chill was upon us, he found the best way to keep her little round body from shivering was to pop her into his oilskin vest. The bond between them has grown, and though she is still only a pup, her natural instinct around sheep is promising. While the other dogs chase a ball or chew a bone, she'll gladly run around and around a nervous flock of guinea fowl or poddy lambs, then lie and watch, and run around and around again. **Carley Walker, Longreach, Qld**

bodies were right at his feet. I think he liked seeing other blokes' dogs beaten up. You wouldn't dare try to rescue your dog because that'd show you thought it was weak. All you could do was to kick the boss's dog or chuck rocks at him out in the paddock when no-one was looking.

Spike sat beside me, surveying the morning dogfights with disdain. When the boss's dog walked up to check him out, Spike's old lips curled, his hackles rose and he let out a fearsome, gravelly growl. The thug froze and retreated. I patted my ugly old bugger's head, but he didn't think he'd done anything special.

For a few months, I didn't get much sheep work. The blokes with proven dogs got most of the yard work and mustering, and although Spike was doing all right with the cattle and enjoyed following my horse all day, no-one had much time for him.

Eventually, I got my chance. Now I don't know if Spike had been watching what the top dogs had been doing, but he worked in the yards like he'd been doing it all his life. He was basically a city dog. He knew about roads and traffic and chasing cats, but here he was leaping rails, speaking up, backing sheep, forcing and staying back just like the best of them. My chest was bursting with pride. The old fellow might have waited until he was ten to work his first sheep, but he never let up, even if it was stinking hot or pelting with rain.

Later on, he moved with me to WA and if I hadn't had such a good dog, I wouldn't have got the jobs I did. In his dotage, Spike sired Louie with the cooperation of one of the station bitches … and this dog surpassed even his great old dad as a worker. Which all goes to show that talent doesn't necessarily need a fancy pedigree.

Some dogs have to do it

Peter Knight Coonabarabran, NSW

It has only been in recent times that Hound has really found his niche in life. It came with the approach of Coonabarabran's annual show and the dog jumping competition. We decided to enter and do a bit of training, but Hound was absolutely hopeless. He just couldn't see any point to it and was not even the slightest bit interested in jumping over anything, unless it was a bitch.

The big day came and time for the big event. I was still caught up at the cattle shed tidying up the last of the Head Steward's jobs, cranky and stroppy as I am allowed to be for that one day. But off I went to make a fool of myself in the main arena. Hound was too busy shaping up to every other dog around to be the slightest bit interested in a stupid dog jumping competition.

The jump was starting to get quite high, but still Hound was more interested in fighting. As long as he was snapped back into reality for long enough to get him confused, we were fine. When I called him from the other side of the jump he just gave a hop and a skip over to the only familiar face he knew. Once we had worked out the psychology of the athlete in Hound, it was hardly a challenge.

Gradually, as the jump grew really big, the competition dropped off and there was less to sidetrack Hound. He actually started to realise what he was supposed to do—and, what's more, enjoy it. You could see he thought it was great fun showing off to everyone as he pranced around, tail high and adrenalin pumping. Besides, he had more attention from me than he had ever had. This was great fun, he reckoned.

I don't think we realised just what it takes out of a dog to be the top dog of Coonabarabran show. Hound pranced around for a bit with his blue ribbon round his neck. He offered a few cursory snarls to the other mere mortals, but you could see his heart was not in it. He made it to the bar with us while we had a celebratory drink but it was all he could do to lift his leg on a log and then curl up and go to sleep. He woke up in time to load the bulls at nine that night, then just slept in the passenger seat all the way home. He couldn't even raise a snarl at the trucks on the highway. It is a tough life but some dogs have to do it.

Hound was one of those dogs for whom the description 'man's best friend' was coined. A great mate, a lot of fun, just occasionally useful and a man wouldn't be without one for quids. He was just one of the many reasons that makes life so worth the pain that is often such a part of living in the bush.

A dog somehow makes it worthwhile to put up with droughts one year then floods the next, prices as low as they can go one year then worse the next. Always there with a smile and never a complaint, may the Hounds of this world continue to help keep the sanity of Australia's rural folk. They work far better than any therapist.

Sentinel duty: my two cattle dogs sit side by side regarding the beautiful view and keeping an eye on any wildlife that might dare come their way. They are best friends and take their sentinel role very seriously. **Mandy Archibald, Murrurundi, NSW**

Working dog at Liveringa Station in Western Australia, after a long day's work in heat 45 degrees plus, right before the wet season.
Kieran and India Woods, Cluan, Tas

Bailed up

Tom Hordacre Tenterden, WA

This happened during the 1930s when I was a schoolboy.

The annual Christmas Tree at the Tenterden Hall was always a big event for the local children. A nearby farmer was to be Father Christmas. My father, being the proud owner of a model T Ford, was asked to pick the old chap up at a pre-arranged point, close to his home.

The appointment was kept by my father. After a few minutes' wait, and no sign of Father Christmas, my father decided to drive up to the farmer's home.

The cause of the delay was immediately obvious. The old gent, dressed in his Father Christmas outfit, was home alone, and frantically waving at the window to draw attention to his normally friendly sheepdog. The dog was loose and, not recognising his master, was holding him prisoner in his own home.

My father managed to calm the dog and chain him up. Father Christmas arrived a little late that year, but was made very welcome by the children.

These two kelpies are bred to use brains and bluff rather than biting needlessly. They are owned by Grant Hutchings at Tenterfield. The leading dog is Karmala Neon, who was born with one brown eye, one blue eye; the blue one changed to a lighter brown as he got older. The bitch is Tracker Gillette, her father is called Glide, and both are aptly named. They are very clever, classy kelpies and keen to work any stock in any conditions. **Jan Lowing, Nobby, Qld**

Winning over the rival

Betty Thompson Bylong, NSW

When I married 43 years ago and came to live with my husband, I felt everything was perfect and the love we had for each other was sublime. Alas, I never dreamt I would have to fight for that love with a dog for two years and be treated with such dislike.

Jinny was my rival right from the very first day I took up my position as a loving wife. She was my husband's shadow and obedient servant, following at his heels wherever he went. There was some doubt about her breeding but she showed a mixture of cattle and sheepdog in her appearance and in her ability to work both cattle and sheep. She was really good to watch, biting as directed by my husband—either just a nip or a really good bite, first one heel and then the other—but she never bit the sheep and was quite handy in the yards as well.

Several months after I married, she still eyed me off with suspicion and would have nothing to do with me. Even when it came to her feed-time she would not accept it from me and would wait until I was out of sight before she very gingerly ate it with distaste. If my husband put his arms around me she would slink off and refuse to follow us another step.

Having lived on the land all my life, I was accustomed to animals and the work associated with them. Naturally I helped with all the outside work when needed, which was often, and especially with the stock. One day I went to help with the muster and, as my own horse was lame, my husband caught one of his horses for me to ride. Normally it was Jinny's habit to spin and bark with excitement, then rush off ahead of us as we mounted. This day, however, as I was about halfway onto the horse, Jinny unwound and, as quick as a flash, darted in and with all her pent-up hatred bit my horse on the front foot. Well, you can just imagine the result. My poor horse let out a wild snort, leapt in the air and at the same time spun sideways. How I managed to land in the saddle remains a mystery to this very day. When I finally quietened my horse and abused the dog, she smirked back at me as if to say, 'I got you that time.'

Her jealousy went on for almost two years and I had given up trying to win her over.

On one occasion we had a bad outbreak of bushfires, and my husband and all the available men had to be on the job both day and night while I was left at home to cope with the chores. We had just begun shearing and had just started into a mob of ewes and lambs and could not stop. As we only had a small two-stand shed, we did the rouseabouting ourselves and, in the absence of my husband and workmen at the fires, I had to turn my talents to being the shed hand.

Jinny was left at home with me and her spirits reached rock-bottom. She went into deep mourning for her master and true love, staying put in her kennel. About the third day, though, she actually followed me to the shed and watched me pick up the

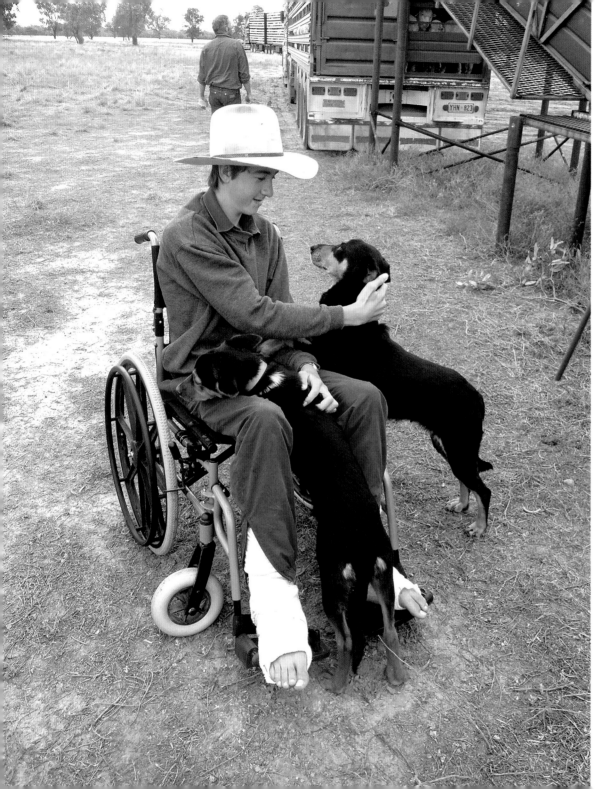

fleeces and throw them on the table and sweep the board. Now and again I gave her a pat and said, 'Cheer up, old girl, he will be home soon.'

Each time there was a small response from her—just a slight wag of the tail—but it was the first ever, and I began to wonder what would happen next.

On the fourth day, she began following me while I did my work inside the shed and when I picked up a fleece, she would pick up a piece of wool, bring it back to the table and drop it at my feet as if to say, 'There, I am helping too.' I would tell her she was a good dog, and get a big tail-wag.

By the end of the week she was keeping close tabs on my every move. She came to help me start the engine to run the generator for our lights at night. As I cranked the motor she would rush in and bark at the handle until it started. Then she would sit down and look at me with her head on one side as if to say, 'There, that helped you get it going, didn't it?'

The final capitulation came when she followed me to bed and slept outside the door all night. I knew at last I was accepted, but I did wonder if she would change when my husband returned.

It was a great surprise that when he finally arrived—exhausted and smelling of smoke and gum leaves—and took me in his arms. She barked her approval, then jumped up and licked, first him, then me.

21

Working overtime

Irene Arnold Tambellup, WA

Our family was watching the television program 'Countrywide' and Skipper, our red kelpie, was lying at our feet.

A close-up of a dog working sheep appeared on the screen and immediately caught his attention. Then, as some sheep went to break away, Skipper rushed forward to head them off.

You should have witnessed the look on his face as he came from behind the television set wondering where the sheep had gone.

Spotty the border collie at eight weeks, contemplating her next move in her attack on the leaves of the old eucalypt in the dog yard. **Kathy Gooch, Pearsondale, Vic**

This is Missy, our ten-month-old working dog, who is still in training on our farm at Wrattonbully, South Australia. Needing much encouragement in her earlier days to get on and off the ute, she now doesn't just hop off the ute as commanded, she launches herself enthusiastically! **Anne Woodard, Naracoorte, SA**

Welcome Home
Ethel Batten Dubbo East, NSW

Bonnie is a black kelpie with a loving nature—and she thinks she is almost human.

When she was about ten months old I was away from home for two weeks in hospital. Upon my return her joy was ecstatic. She showed her loving welcome and her pleasure at seeing me by racing around me and about the gardens and trees, tail tucked under, ears up, eyes bright, tongue lolling from a big toothy grin.

On her last lap under the grapevines she paused to snatch off a bunch of grapes and placed them on my foot. It was truly a marvellous welcome home from a loving friend. It made me cry!

On automatic

Bill Franklin Cowell, SA

Our border collie, Bob, was a great sheepdog, but he was good with the house cow too.

Every day, Bob would go and fetch the cow whenever he heard the rattle of the milk bucket. By the time one of us had walked from the house to the milking shed 300 metres away, Bob would have the cow waiting in the yard.

One morning, however, some months after we had sold the house cow, I had reason to use the old milk bucket. I was amazed when, about half an hour later, Bob turned up with the Jersey from the adjoining farm two kilometres away.

On the road with a mob of cattle, Jack, Delta, Duke and Spike are ready for any eventuality. Owner Hamish Mitchell from Kingstown in northern New South Wales had a big mob on the road for several months during the drought of 2005. His dogs were a vital part of the team, and here they are waiting for the next job. Without the dogs it would be impossible to manage the cattle—dogs can easily get cattle out of difficult areas, whereas a horse or quad bike can't. **Hamish Mitchell**; photo sent in by **Phil Irvine, Yarrowyck, NSW**

Wedded bliss

Marj Wood Benalla, Vic

Skipper was married to the boss long before I was. He wasn't very thrilled with my arrival and made sure I knew that the boss was his. In Skipper's opinion the management order was the boss, Skipper and 'her', a very poor third.

Early in our marriage I used to love riding in the back of the ute, with the cold wind blowing in my face as we roared along the narrow dirt roads. Skipper refused to ride in the back with 'her', choosing instead to sit on the passenger seat next to the boss.

When the stock crate was on the back of the ute, I'd squeeze through the gate and into the back, while Skipper sat disdainfully in the front.

Seeing the ute go past with the boss's wife inside the stock crate and his dog up front beside him, the locals decided that here was one farmer who had his priorities right.

Walking across the paddock at dusk. **Nicole Harwood, Cunderin, WA**

Pip, the marriage broker

Susan Martel Gollan, NSW

My childhood memories of Pip are of an aged brown kelpie. Yet it is to Pip I owe my existence. It was he who sealed my parents' relationship.

Pip was my father's favourite dog. Dad, a young bachelor manager, had obtained Pip as soon as he returned from active duties in World War II. Pip was his mate and worked with him through drought, flood and ordinary times.

Mother, a tall, dark-haired, attractive young lady, was swept off her feet at the local Bachelors and Spinsters Ball by the handsome manager who, at 33, had somehow managed to avoid matrimony.

As young men of the land often do, Dad had taken Pip when courting Mother, who worked at her father's stock and station agency. I often wonder what Mother thought of this since, as I remember, she did not appear to be over-fond of dogs. I recall that she wouldn't let us bring the dogs into the house, take them in the car or even allow them into the garden. Yet when family discussions turned to the worth of dogs, even Mum would become a little misty-eyed when Pip was remembered.

It was not until my parents' fortieth wedding anniversary three years ago that I learnt why Pip was such a popular dog. Dad related the story.

One morning at the property where he worked, some 30 miles from town, he came out to discover that Pip was nowhere to be seen. All staff were alerted to keep an eye out for Pip, since dogs die quickly from snakebite.

That night, Dad received a phone call. Pip had turned up at Mother's family home. What a good excuse to go to town! Dad happily drove the 30 miles of potholed road to retrieve Pip.

He seemed to be convinced that for Pip to walk 30 miles, he must have been trying to drop some hint about the stock agent's beautiful daughter. So Dad did the only sensible thing and asked for Mother's hand, there and then.

Tully loves being out with the other animals on our property. If we are not working the sheep she is most often found sitting in the horse yard, watching the two Jindabyne brumbies. **Karen Davis, Muswellbrook, NSW**

One yell too many

Tresna Shorter Katherine, NT

Bond, two-year-old border collie, head sheepdog at Bluemoon, Jugiong, New South Wales. **Jason McFarlane**; photo sent in by **Deb Kelly, Jugiong, NSW**

Despite his lack of training, Fella, being a border collie, had natural ability and knew instinctively what to do. This was more than could be said for the rest of us. My husband, who was more interested in wheat growing than dealing with animals, had little patience when it came to sheep.

In his impatience, it was not long before he started yelling at all of us for not being in the right place at the right time. I could take being yelled at a couple of times, but being a city girl and still learning country ways, I soon became annoyed. After all, I reasoned, we were helping him out during a labour shortage, weren't we? Where would he be without us? Foolishly, I expected gratitude, not abuse.

Eventually, he yelled at me one time too many and I turned around and started walking home. Next, he yelled at Fella, and to our amazement, Fella also turned and strutted home across the paddock with his crooked tail waving in the air.

Later, my husband had a good laugh that even the dog wouldn't put up with his rotten temper.

33

Not on speaking terms

Denis Adams Apsley, Vic

Our dogs (from left to right): Sally (border collie), Cindy (coolie cross border collie), Jazz (coolie cross kelpie), Coolie (coolie), Smokey (Australian kelpie) and Zac (kelpie). They are all part of our family and all help on the farm; some are better at helping than others. We have a cage on the back of the ute to carry them safely between properties. They all want to come along, and it's a five-minute job to get them all on board, as three of them need to be lifted up. We just love their happy smiling faces! **Steinfort family, Katunga, Vic**

When I went to Jabuk in 1952, one of our neighbours was Alan Ross, a man ahead of his time in the control of sand drift. He was one of the nicest blokes you'd ever meet, but even old Alan could be temporarily unpopular.

One day I found him hard at work in the sheep yards. And 'hard' was the operative word. Normally his large, plump sheepdog bitch Trixie did just about everything except work the drafting gate. This day, however, Trixie was not her usual, busy self. She was acting like a wife whose husband had forgotten her birthday.

She would half fill the yard, then pause to give Alan a dirty look.

'Come on, Trixie,' he would urge. Then, with a look that plainly said 'Humph', she would disdainfully run a few more in.

'What's up with Trixie?' I asked.

'Oh, she's not speaking to me today,' Alan told me, looking embarrassed. 'You know how humid and stinking hot it was yesterday, before we had that bit of a thunderstorm? Well, I was feeling so tired and crook with this damn boil on my backside, I thought I'd take a spell. I was lying on my belly out on the bed on the verandah.'

Coming from Alan, this was an amazing admission. Normally he ran rings around all us young blokes. He was a bit of a workaholic.

'Trixie was asleep under the bed,' he went on. 'Then all of a sudden there was a terrific clap of thunder. She got such a scare that she jumped up on top of me—fair on my boil!'

Alan, it seemed, had risen vertically some distance above the bed. With a howl of agony, he had lashed out instinctively at poor, terrified Trixie.

'I didn't mean to kick the old girl,' he told me sadly. 'I was sorry as soon as I'd done it, but she still hasn't forgiven me!'

35

Tough country, tough dogs

Peter Clarke Kununurra, WA

I used to work as overseer on Tubbo Station in the New South Wales Riverina. Tubbo was sheepdog paradise with up to 35,000 merino sheep of fine quality.

There were good-sized paddocks for the dogs to have a decent cast around, big yards, big numbers and big mobs. The Tubbo woolshed is 102 stands and to fill her up with 3,000 woolly sheep, good dogs were needed. Many a time I saw old Bob's dog Humphrey back a running mob of wethers 200 yards up through the yards and way through the shed, turn round and back them in the other direction as they ran in.

Sheepdogs! The outstation overseer ran anywhere between fourteen and nineteen dogs at once. His ute was a mobile dog kennel, with kelpies, border collie crosses and the odd pure collie thrown in—all different sizes, different ages, and different levels of ability.

The ute sides were strung with roo legs and old sheep that made up the tucker for these dogs. His job involved a lot of droving and mustering of lines of sheep of similar age from various paddocks into one mob and taking them the 30 miles into the shed. Mobs of 4,000 were common and even bigger mobs of 12,000 weaners were handled by dogs on Tubbo.

It is a skilful team of man and dog that can count through a gate 3,000 to 4,000 sheep, keep tallies, direct the odd young dog and keep the ants out of one's boots all at once.

A dog is a man's best friend. My top dog was a kelpie-New Zealand border collie bitch called Lucy. Sheep were her life. In winter when the ice was on the puddles, she'd have a good swim, then jump up on the ute ready for work.

She would sit on a whistle or wave of a hand away across the paddock. She would work on a wing or tail a mob for miles with no directions. She worked on when her body wanted to stop—130 degrees or more in the sun, pads worn and cracked and troughs miles apart, but she never let me down. Never. She was my friend and my helper. I couldn't have done the job with only my four dogs if Lucy wasn't there. A dog is worth five men and Lucy worth five dogs.

I told her through a veil of tears how much I loved her as I buried her.

On my family's cattle station in the south-west Pilbara, my team of kelpies are never far away and always ready for the next job to start. The positive effect our working dogs have had on our stock is undeniable, with ease of handling during mustering being a standout improvement, especially in our weaners. As well as being an essential part of our weaner handling program, their companionship and role as my trusty sidekicks are equally appreciated. I couldn't imagine life without them now. **Aticia Grey, Glenflorrie Station, WA**

One of the last photos of Ralphy, our kelpie cross huntaway (nearest Ben), before he was tragically taken from us by a snake bite. Working with Ralphy's very best friend in the world is Bandit, our kelpie cross border collie cross blue heeler. And Raylene, our red cloud, who in her retirement is now living a ridiculously comfortable life on our loungeroom couch. In this photo they are doing their best to help Ben move a mob into the drafting race. At the end of this day it was decided that Bandit—being easily distracted, so better suited to catching butterflies rather than doing sheep work—would become a house dog. **Felicity Mead, Boyup Brook, WA**

Life in a pit
Stephen Vagg Barmera, SA

An ex-livestock transport driver living at Burra in South Australia's mid-north walked from his house one day to find both of his kelpie dogs showing signs of having eaten snail bait, which unfortunately had been left lying around.

The old dog was near death. The younger pup, however, didn't appear to be so bad. On phoning the nearest vet at Clare, the owner was advised to bring the pup to the surgery immediately.

On the way, he briefly stopped at the saleyards and 'finished off' the old dog with a humane blow to the head with a large shifting spanner. He left him in a pit used for disposing of dead sheep. The pup was then taken on to the vet and, following treatment, duly recovered.

Twelve months or so later, while at the Burra sheep sales, the dog owner noticed a familiar-looking kelpie working sheep. He asked a fellow truck driver where he had acquired the dog.

The new owner said he had come across the dog about a year before, trying to extricate itself from the sheep pit in which it had been left, presumed dead. After the original owner explained the situation, the dog was returned to him, none the worse for the experience except for a permanent lump on the head.

Subsequent discussions with the vet indicated that the blow to the head may have saved the dog's life as during unconsciousness its system slowed, possibly providing better resistance to the poison.

39

Jenny Molloy and her two loyal helpers, Fly and Ollie, at the family farm in Harrogate, South Australia. **Sally Harding, Albury, NSW**

Thirsty fellow

Beryl Parish Stuarts Point, NSW

We had a cattle dog called Sam, a border collie–kelpie cross. He always followed my husband to the yard when he milked the house cow. My husband would always squirt some milk into an icecream container for the animals after he had enough for the household. Sam would have a drink and then the rest was brought to the house for the cat. When the container was empty it was left at the back gate for the next day.

One afternoon Sam must have got thirsty because I looked out the window and saw him pick up the container in his mouth and take it out to where the house cow was feeding and put it under her udder. Then he sat and waited, but she walked on after a few seconds. Not to be outdone, Sam picked up the container again, followed the cow and did the same thing. She didn't understand of course, and kept walking away until Sam gave up.

Some of my sheepdog trialling dogs and also my faithful retired kelpies. My first working dog was the old kelpie, Dash. She is a tough dog that gives all her heart in any job she is doing. She started my interest in sheepdogs. I did my first three sheepdog trials with Cricket, the younger kelpie, many years ago. She started well and has a soft way with sheep. Unfortunately too soft. She seems to prefer the role of guardian of sheep and escorts baby lambs around the paddock, often engaging in games of tag with them. At least she keeps foxes away. My first working border collie, Abby, has been a great teacher for me. She has a natural way with sheep and enabled me to get really interested in the sport. Once bitten by the trialling bug, one dog just wasn't enough! As pups take a while to raise and train I purchased a started dog, Teisha, who gave us some extra challenges as she is white. I've bred a litter out of each of them and kept a pup or two, training them to become a team that works together. **Alison Burrell, Nelson, NSW**

Kobie, heading for an afternoon swim. **Gregory Brown, Maldon, Vic**

Oh! What a feeling

Doug Keith Elmhurst, Vic

The tray of the Hilux ute was rusting away, mainly due to the male dogs using it as a urinal. I purchased an aluminium tray as a replacement and put it into storage for the time being.

In due course, when there were no other urgent jobs, I parked the ute near the workshop and set about removing the old tray.

The dogs dozed in the sun, occasionally opening one eye to make sure that they weren't missing anything important, but generally conserving energy until there was some real action.

Eventually all the rusted bolts were undone and I removed the old tray from the chassis, and dragged it some twenty feet away. I then got into the cab to go and collect the replacement tray.

Instant action from the dogs! Decisions to be made! In an instant, habit took over and all four dogs dashed for the old tray and leapt on. Oh! What a feeling!

But as I drove away, their euphoria evaporated and you could see their expressions change to—'Trust a bloody Toyota to fall in half just when we're needed!'.

Six months across the gulf

Dick Mills Kanmantoo, SA

A few years prior to the First World War, my grandfather, WG Mills, MHR, assisted his second son, Richard, to purchase a property near Elbow Hill, south of Cowell on Eyre Peninsula.

Alec, my father, was to take a flock of sheep from our place at Millbrae near Kanmantoo in the Adelaide Hills over to Cowell to stock the place. Alec was seventeen or eighteen years old at the time.

The sheep were driven by him on foot with a dog called Shep to Port Adelaide, then loaded aboard a barge to go around the tip of Yorke Peninsula and up Spencer Gulf to Franklin Harbour at Cowell. Then they again had to travel on foot to the farm down along the coast.

Shep had plenty of fuss made of him when finally the paddock gate was shut. It had been a long, slow trip. Shep, however, was to be left behind to give Richard a hand, as well as some company.

After a few days' stay to look around the new farm, Alec returned by ship to Port Adelaide. And then on to Millbrae.

Soon after Alec left, Shep disappeared. Alec got the news in a letter from Richard and resigned himself to the loss of another good dog, a not uncommon occurrence. New dogs were constantly being bred and trained for that reason.

Time passed. Winter came bringing green grass in the paddocks and the cries of newborn lambs across the valley. Lamb-tailing passed, then shearing.

One bright morning, Alec opened the back door and there, wagging his tail and grinning with great joy, was Shep. Everyone was amazed that a dog could find his way home across two gulfs.

It had taken him six months.

Gus has his first beach experience at Point Hut on the Murrumbidgee River. **Bill Russo, Longueville, NSW**

Chance

Robert Ellis Duckmaloi via Oberon, NSW

In 1941 my father went to war. He was in the 8th Division which was devastated during the fall of Singapore. He was among those killed.

He had a two-tone tan kelpie dog named Chance, who besides being a good sheepdog was also Dad's very good mate. We were then living on Round Hill, a property at Eugowra owned by my uncle. Round Hill was three miles from Eugowra. The railway line went through the property.

Each day a train travelled from Cowra to Eugowra, arriving at 9.30 am and departing at 4 pm for the return journey. When he left for the war, Dad boarded this train, leaving from a point at Round Hill where his family and dog saw him off. I was not yet one year of age.

We lived for a further two years at Round Hill, where each day Chance went down to the spot where my father boarded the train. He always left, rain, hail or shine, just on 4 pm and arrived just before the train went past. He stayed there for a further ten or fifteen minutes before returning home.

He wouldn't work for my uncle or anyone else after Dad had gone.

Two years later we shifted into town, where, again when loose, he left our house about 3.30 pm and trotted along the railway track until he came to the site where he last saw Dad. He would lie down waiting for the train to go past.

After it had passed, he waited about ten minutes, looking down the track, and then slowly trotted off home again.

This went on for a further three years until one day, old and sick, he didn't return.

He was found dead, where he last saw my Dad.

I still have descendants of Chance today. They display the same devotion.

Sam knew

R.D. McDonald Kerang, Vic

I cannot let the chance go by without telling this story of Sam. Now, I am not a writer or storyteller by nature, but I will put the true facts on paper and I think people might find them interesting.

Very early in the 1930s Depression, three young men decided to get out of Melbourne and all its troubles. One of these young men had worked in our district, so they made it their destination. They bought a horse and buggy, which were very cheap in those days, and off they set, seeking casual work and food as they travelled the 280 kilometres north.

One landowner gave them a dog for company. This was fine until they passed a paddock with sheep near the fence. The dog straightaway went quietly around the sheep and herded them to the roadside in quite good style. The dog kept doing the same thing each time they were near sheep.

When they reached our area, we were shearing and they did some casual work around the shed. I took notice of the dog and was impressed by his ability. I eventually offered them five pounds for him and they were delighted as five pounds was a lot of money in 1931.

The spokesman for the three was Sam Felling, so I named the dog Sam. Then his real work began. We quickly became attached and he would not let me out of his sight.

We had a property 30 miles away from the home property and I used to do most of the sheep work there. To muster this property meant riding the 30 miles with Sam trotting along at the horse's heels. Sam then would muster and help draft the sheep, never turning a hair. If necessary, he would follow me home that evening. He was truly a great working dog and he loved it. However, there were plenty of good working dogs. The real part of the story is as follows.

When war broke out in September of 1939. I immediately joined the forces. I went into camp in October 1939, which meant that I quickly had to place Sam in good hands. My elder brother was glad to take care of him.

Knowing that Sam was very much a one-man dog, my brother kept him well tied up until he got settled, before taking him around the sheep. Sam gradually adapted and seemed to like his new environment.

The old soul, Louis. A true protector, man's best friend and working dog. Looking over the farm as a new day rises.
Breanna Gregory, Pinnaroo, SA

I was away for nearly three years from when I first took Sam to my brother. Sam by this time was quite at home there.

After returning from the Middle East, we got a few days' leave to go home. I arrived late one Friday night and after greeting my family I enjoyed the strange luxury of a comfortable bed.

I woke early in the morning and was anxious to get out and look around. When I opened the back door, there was Sam on the mat. He looked at me a little guiltily, but as soon as I spoke and patted him, he was all over me, and until I delivered him back to my brother, he was glued to my heels.

To get to our place, Sam would have had to travel nearly 40 miles if he'd followed the roads. If he'd gone as the crow flies, it was at least 25 miles and he would have had to swim two major streams—the Murray and the Little Murray—and go through heavy red gum forests.

This was quite an achievement, apart from the timing of it all. It made me wonder if he had been uneasy when we were pinned down by shellfire in the desert, or bombed and strafed at.

I know I probably haven't told this very well, but now I feel too sentimental to rewrite it or say any more.

49

Not the best dog in Highbury

Geoffrey Blight Narrogin, WA

Standing on the side of the road on a cool April afternoon never struck me as being the place I might hear a great dog story. So when a familiar ute pulled up as I herded a mob of crutched weaners into the paddock, I hardly could have guessed the outcome.

It was old Bill. I'd known him all my life. He was of my father's generation and Dad's mate. Dad's been gone ten years and I'm a grandfather, so old Bill is no longer young.

Bill never married. A very shy chap, I'd had many talks with him over the years.

'I've been reading your yarns,' he said.

I sensed there was something more. Bill wasn't the reading type, but as we talked he again came back to the dog story of mine he'd read.

'If I tell you a dog story, you won't laugh, will you?'

He didn't have to ask.

'I haven't told anyone in fifty years, but you might be able to tell me why it happened.'

Bill's old face, wrinkled with age, almost blushed and I wondered at his shyness.

Bill was the last of a family that had pioneered Highbury. We had buried his brother a fortnight before.

'Your uncle gave me a dog once,' he began. 'A black kelpie called Jack. Not the best sheepdog in Highbury, but he did me and we got on all right.'

The story I now repeat was told uninterrupted on the side of a gravel track that fifty years before had seen Bill, his old dad and Jack travel four miles to the Highbury siding at midnight. There Bill caught the train and went to war.

His kelpie Jack was his only possession and his dad promised to look after the wayward old mutt. He told Bill to take care and to come home as soon as he could. Bill stood at the train window and stared at the old ute's fading lights. He was filled with restlessness and fear as he left his father and dog in that dark railway yard.

Bill had mates going also. Soon the homesickness gave way to a sense of adventure. The whole world was before them, but not for long. War makes young men grow up fast and Bill was no different. He soon learnt about the fear and tragedy of the cost of lives. Unlike the others, he didn't have a girl back home, making him feel left out when the blokes spoke of getting back to their women. He used to think of old Jack and wonder how he was going.

His mother sent letters. There weren't many. They told him Jack was still Jack, still no better at rounding up sheep. Things seemed to be always grim. It was who had fallen or been injured, or how terrible the grain and wool prices were. But—they were from home.

Bill lost a close mate. Everybody did. There was no-one to tell. He wondered why he was there. He was sent to Queensland for retraining for the jungle. The Allied position was bad. The Japanese were advancing through New Guinea and already bombing Darwin. It looked like a certain attack on Australia.

Bill had not had home leave for years. Suddenly, he was told to go home and see his folks before being sent to the Islands. Not permitted to tell anybody, nor allowed to write or phone, he was issued rail passes for travel. The Defence Force didn't want troop movements known or recorded anywhere. It took Bill eleven days to get on the 'Midnight Horror' that would take him home to Highbury. Everybody was frightened and depressed. The war was going badly.

Even though he had been travelling for eleven days, it seemed an eternity to wait at Narrogin station. The people had a midnight cuppa and the slow Albany train passed through on its way to Perth. The trains always passed each other at Narrogin, so the first there had to wait.

Finally they were rolling again. Bill stood in the rocking gangway looking out into the gloom, knowing that only a mile further was home—and Jack. It had been too long. No light showed in the darkness.

The red and tan dog is Gogetta BoDuke. He is two years old and every day he waits patiently on the back of the ute for his boss. He is loyal, trustworthy, and clever on his feet. He has wonderful anticipation of stock movement and is in position before the break. He loves belly rubs and cuddles with our son and is sometimes found on the couch. He continues to be a wonderful team member and mate, and we couldn't ask for a better dog. **Luke and Zoe Crouch, Hensley Park, Vic**

Suddenly Bill felt good. He was nearly home. He realised that he would have to walk back four miles, but what the hell. There weren't any guns here. Not yet, anyway. How great it would be to see his parents and Jack. God, I hope he's still alive, thought Bill. He would be old now for a dog.

There were no lights in Highbury. No-one to meet the train. The train slowed and finally halted as the guard, with a lantern, jumped down to drop a solitary parcel. Bill jumped down into the darkness. There was no platform. The train immediately shuddered and began its slow choo, choo, choo before slipping away into the night. Suddenly Bill lived a magic moment of his life. One he has never forgotten. It led him down the road to tell me fifty years later. About the dog who wasn't the best sheepdog in Highbury. The dog that jumped up to greet him in the pitch darkness that night and embrace him.

Bill was never an emotional man. Very much the opposite. Never one to have admitted a tear, but on this occasion, even as he told me fifty years later, his eyes glistened as he remembered.

'You know, I'm glad no-one was watching. I couldn't help it. I broke down and cried. You know that bloody dog was worth fighting for.'

Although he asked discreetly later, nobody had ever seen Jack in Highbury. No-one knew whether he was there when the midnight trains came in. It was four miles to where he lived.

'How was it?' asked Bill. 'How did he know I was coming home?'

'Another funny thing,' Bill went on, 'after I walked home with Jack, I didn't wake the parents. I just went off to my room and went to bed. At daylight, Dad came in carrying a cup of tea.'

'I knew you were home the minute I saw old Jack this morning,' was his quiet way of saying 'Welcome home, son'.

Bill said, 'He would never tell me why he made the cup of tea before checking, or whether he had ever brought over a cuppa when I wasn't home.'

Those were secrets Bill's father died with.

'That's why I never told anyone about Jack,' Bill said. 'I don't think they would have believed me.'

Just you try and get past me. Smokey the black kelpie keeps the Dorpers pushed up in the yards. It's all in a day's work, and he loves it. **Julie M Bennett, Stoneleigh, Vic**

The very last lap

D H Turnbull Cleve, SA

As a young man I spent many long hours driving a horse team to clear a scrub block.

My black and white border collie, Spotty, would come out in the morning behind the team and follow for the first round of the paddock. He would then spend the rest of the day sitting around the lunch box or sniffing out rabbits.

Then, with some uncanny sense of timing, he would follow the team for the very last lap of the paddock before knock-off time. Only once did he make a mistake and have to do two laps.

Pride's short cut

Phillip Clerici Sale, Vic

During the 1930s, my late father-in-law, Arthur Taylor, then proprietor of the Ensay Transport Service in far East Gippsland, had a kelpie cross named Pride. The dog had been a bit of a champion in his day.

One day Arthur and Pride unloaded a few sheep near the transport depot for transfer to the saleyards just around the corner.

The local pub, The Little River Inn, was en route to the saleyards, so Arthur popped in for a quick glass, leaving Pride to attend to the sheep.

Pride must have felt left out, because he directed the sheep through the front door of the pub and headed for the bar. However, the bar door was closed, so he continued with the sheep down the passage, through the hotel and out the back door. He continued on to the saleyards after his 'short cut' without losing any of his charges.

A lust for work

H J Treasure Cowra, NSW

I have never known a dog to enjoy his work so much. When it was over you felt like apologising to him. Choc had the look of a deflated balloon as he slunk away to his kennel to wait for the next job to begin. While waiting, he always lay with his feet crossed like an old man. I don't know if this was body language for confidence or some other thing. But he always did it.

Choc could move across a sheep's back with the footwork of a dancer, or move under their bellies like a half-back breaking from the scrum base. He would use his front paws like hands, loading sheep. And as he grew older and stronger, he used his shoulders too.

Single out a sheep in the mob and he could catch it. His eyes would never leave the animal after he had singled it out. Find a lamb on the wrong side of a fence and he would stay there all day if necessary to guard it, belly low to the ground and eyes never off the face. Pick up a knife and sharpening stone and the killers would be under your feet in a few moments.

They say a dog is man's best friend. When things are going wrong, as they sometimes do on the land, the dog often seems to sense it and stands as close to you as he can. Then he'll sit on your boot and lean against your leg to get a little closer. Somehow this always seems to make things a little easier.

One of my biggest joys of owning sheepdogs is watching their development. Starting off with a pup that wants to charge in and chase anything that moves, you slowly develop and train him or her into whatever you desire of your best pal. Through endless training sessions and some very frustrating times, you eventually get to the point where they become one of the biggest assets to any farm. If you take a step back and watch them work you will see just how much they love it, and the pure joy on their faces as they work is something that makes the hours of frustration with a young pup worth it. **Sam Sullivan, Coonabarabran, NSW**

In 1995 I was driving between Adelaide and Wagga Wagga. As I passed through Tanunda, South Australia, I just had to stop and chat with the owner of this lot of coolies. It was one of those unique occasions where a rural representation of the locality is on show in the main street, in bulk. Norm was the gentleman's name; from memory, he said that the coolies were working dogs on various properties throughout the district. The dogs were all very controlled while in the ute and were extremely accommodating in posing for photos. Their gaze followed me as I moved around the ute to improve my angles.
Greg White, Kurrajong Heights, NSW

Sunday stowaway

Beth Henke Mumbannar, Vic

It is extraordinary what lengths your best friend will go to so she, too, can go visiting on a Sunday afternoon—despite having been told to stay home. Wocky, our blue heeler cross, was as broad as she was tall and reckoned she knew as much as her boss. On this occasion, she outsmarted even him.

We set off in our old XR Falcon ute to journey across country to the parents-in-law for the afternoon. Wocky was determined to be part of the visit. She came with us to the first gate, but was growled at and told to stay home. We shut the gate and when we couldn't see her, didn't think much more of it. We thought she had slunk off through the rushes and swamp for home.

We travelled on, opening and closing seven gates. We stopped to change a flat tyre but then continued on across country and into a pine forest. We were stopped there by tourists who asked questions about the lie of the land. Suddenly the old XR died. We opened the bonnet to investigate the problem—and there was determined old Wocky, sitting between the engine and the mudguard.

The tourists looked a little stunned, but the boss just casually remarked, 'Oh, that's where we carry our dogs in this part of the bush.'

In her keenness to meet the tourists' labradors after her cramped and bumpy journey of twenty miles, she had wriggled the petrol pipe off the engine block.

100 miles back to Pata

Ruth Payne Victor Harbor, SA

We were living on a farm at Pata, near Loxton. Our boss had a mob of sheep on a property at Pompoota, near Murray Bridge, which he checked regularly with the help of his dog Tinker.

One day, the boss went to Pompoota and decided to sell the sheep at the next market. He left his dog with a neighbour until his return.

Back home at Pata, he was up early next morning to do the milking. He missed his usual helper, but out of habit called him anyway, saying, 'Fetch the cows, Tink!'

He was utterly amazed when out from a sheltering bush crept his faithful dog—footsore and weary but ready to work. Tinker hadn't liked the idea of being left behind, so had walked 100 miles overnight to get home.

In the sheep yards there's always one flighty lamb or ewe that decides to be difficult and challenge the dog. With a quick spring in her step, Jade is able to change direction and head the lamb off before it comes back flying into the fence or, worse, into my legs. Even the most stubborn sheep will always try to push the dog as far as they can. But if you have a dog that can handle the situation, he or she will always come out on top, which can save a lot of time and energy for yourself. **Sam Sullivan, Coonabarabran, NSW**

Repaid in full

Mavis Appleyard Warren, NSW

When he was sixteen, my husband Doug found a man ill-treating a young kelpie bitch. After an altercation he took the dog with him and kept her.

He called her Janet and she filled the void in the lonely life he led on a huge sheep station. She quickly became a wonderful, reliable worker, mustering huge paddocks, drafting, penning up, yarding and doing shed work. She knew what to do before she was even told to do it and Doug and she were inseparable.

One day working in the shed at Butterbone Stud Park, Doug was frantically busy and starting to get very annoyed with Janet because she kept disappearing. She had to be repeatedly called from under the shearing shed.

By nightfall when he knocked off, Doug was exasperated with her and she finally crept out looking very guilty after much angry calling. In the eight years he had owned her, she had never let him down or left his side when they were working. When she made it obvious she wanted him to check under the shed, he did. In a corner, where the sheep penned under the shed could not walk on them, were thirteen newborn pups that she had produced between taking mobs in, yarding, penning up and taking sheep away.

Janet repaid us in thousands of ways in her thirteen years for being rescued from a cruel owner. She was a very shy dog and did not like children near her, generally giving them a wide berth. However, after a lot of rain I couldn't find our fifteen-month-old son. Hearing his annoyed squeals from near the swollen creek, I ran down there and found Janet running between him and the water, bumping him sideways away from the water.

She looked very relieved to see me and quickly disappeared to leave me to collect him.

Getting acquainted

Geraldine Boylan Port Lincoln, SA

Between 1988 and 1991, I worked as a counsellor with rural communities. Having been raised as farm girl I was well versed in the position held by the farm dog.

On arrival at a farm I developed the habit of winding down my car window and spending time quietly getting acquainted with the 'Boss' of the farm or with the 'Boss and his or her supporters'. They never let me down. They always rolled up to give me the once-over.

I learned much from observing these dogs. Sometimes I established a relationship quickly. A few words had them literally eating from my hand. At other times the inspection was more comprehensive—the wheels received the usual 'sniff and wee' treatment before I was given so much as a stare. Once the look in their eyes went from watchful to mellow, I learned to open the door and to sit quietly and allow the personal inspection. Mostly I found that after sniffs and a few licks, I'd made the grade.

After a while I learned to place the dogs in three categories— the wary, the smoochers and the rude. The wary dog often remained aloof, watchful and tense until I earned his acceptance. With quiet talking this dog could eventually be won over. I remember one occasion when I sat in the car and calmly explained the purpose of my visit to the dog. I explained I was not the bank manager. At that moment a head came around the shed corner and a voice said, 'I'm glad about that. I wasn't coming out—until I heard you say that.'

The smoochers were pushover dogs. Thank goodness they were in plentiful supply. My relations with them were mutually satisfying.

Sadly, I found there were more rude dogs on farms than any other types. They seemed to take great delight in actions which defied all words and which rendered unexpected and immediate embarrassment.

But in a way I respected these rude dogs. Their instincts still ruled supreme, despite their training and complex skills. Even though they were totally obedient and submissive to a boss in the paddock, they were still masters of themselves. Politeness, the mark of civilised society, could never be trained into these dogs. They had everyone at their mercy. Any visitor with a superior air and an expensive suit could be humbled with a good sniff in the crutch.

Farm dogs often made it clear what was going on, what was the state of the bank balance and how depressed their owners. If a farm was falling to pieces you'd often find half a dead sheep dragged on to the verandah, holes dug all around the house and dogs and their mess lying around everywhere. There'd be a general air of decay as the dogs extended their territory into that of their owners, who no longer were able to take an interest in disciplining their dogs and drawing boundaries between dog and human.

You could see loneliness in the eyes of these dogs. They were no longer working—all the stock had gone. They were starved for company as the wives were out working and the kids had left home to look for work in the city.

There was an air of resignation in a lot of these dogs' eyes. They'd throw themselves at you with a sort of desperate joyfulness, happy to have company, but looking for leadership and purpose once more to their lives.

Meet Eddie, Mr Personality Plus, an eighteen-month-old kelpie who works on a farm on the far north coast of New South Wales. He lives for five things: rounding up cattle, barking at cattle, chasing cattle, watching cattle and retrieving sticks. It seems Eddie also believes he has a future as a motorbike stunt rider, rodeo clown and part-time model. As well as being an excellent work dog, Eddie reinforces the saying 'a dog is man's best mate'.
**Amy Schiller,
Murwillumbah, NSW**

In a state of shock

Malcolm Seymour Miling, WA

My black and tan kelpie was eleven months old at the time of this story and was spending a lot of time with me as part of his training. During the day, between spells on the header and trips to the silo with the wheat trucks, he would sleep on the passenger-side floor of the utility.

Harvesting a long, narrow, sand-plain paddock next to a shire road one day, I noticed as I came around the top corner that the header steering was not normal. One of the back tyres was half flat due to straw stuck in the valve. Since it was too flat to carry on with, I had to walk about one kilometre to the other end of the paddock where the truck and ute were parked next to a gate leading onto the road. I drove the utility, which had the compressor on the tray, back to the header to blow the tyre up again.

That being done, I was then faced with the problem of returning the ute to the other end of the paddock and another long walk. Because the paddock was clear, I decided to point the ute straight at the truck, put it in low-range first gear, and let it get there at snail pace on its own. I tied the steering wheel to the seat springs and set it on its way.

Carrying on with the header, I watched the progress of the ute to ensure I was near the truck when it arrived. As I went past it, I saw that the dog, who had been asleep on the floor, had woken and jumped up onto the driver's seat to see what was happening. I was getting close to the truck with a header bin nearly full of wheat when I noticed that a car had pulled in off the road and a salesman was standing waiting for the ute to arrive so he could tell the driver all about his product.

I stopped at the truck and left the header unloading to walk over to the ute which was just arriving. The dog was sitting in the driver's seat, front paws on the steering wheel, being watched by the salesman, who had just realised the dog was apparently in full control. Opening the door, I pushed the gears out and turned the engine off. I casually remarked to the surprised onlooker that, although the dog drove quite well, he wasn't heavy enough to work the clutch, so I had to start and stop the ute for him. Conscious of the header unloading, I quickly found out what product the salesman was selling, decided we didn't need any, hopped back on the header and carried on harvesting.

The salesman, who was a stranger to the district, appeared to be suffering from mild shock as he slowly drove off.

From bringing in the sheep for shearing, to mustering ewes and lambs, my trusty work dogs are always close at hand. They never complain and are always glad to see me. A pat on the back, a juicy bone and a warm snug bed at the end of the day is all the reward they ever want. **Karyn Buller, Darkan, WA**

Celebrity on the roof

Blanche Niemann Mildura, Vic

Growing up on a south-western Riverina wool property called Mindook station provided me with many, many wonderful memories—the country, the river, the lifestyle and especially the animals.

Looking back on my childhood, no memory is stronger or more vivid than that of our gallant sheepdog, Pudden—a legend, a friend and an outstanding working dog. He had been a soft, wriggly, licky puppy, coloured grey, black and many other earthy colours all mixed together, with one blue and one brown eye. He learnt fast, displaying the intelligence of the German coolie breed and the gentle demeanour of his kelpie cross. He watched the other dogs and copied—but a raised voice was enough to send him scurrying away, tail tucked between his legs, not to be seen again until the heat had passed.

He was my father's shadow, never to be found far from him. As he grew older, his personality also began to develop. He took up the unusual habit of travelling on the roof of the farm ute. He would leap into the back of the ute, then bounce up onto the roof, legs braced against the rough country roads. He wasn't even discouraged by highway travel—nose pointed straight ahead, and ears flapping in the wind. He became quite a celebrity in the district. Truckies tooted as they passed and described his antics to their mates over their CBs.

The tin roof of the Suzuki ute started to sag. Cracks appeared and rain cascaded into the cabin. The local garage owner knew Pud was a committed roof rider, so he designed and built a cover for the cabin that was a bit more sturdy, and kept out the rain.

After a rendezvous with the neighbour's bitch, he was delivered home, standing proudly on the roof of Mr Murphy's new Commodore. The scratches in the royal blue duco hardly showed, but the tension on Murphy's face was evident.

As older dogs died, Pud stood alone as 'the only dog worth his salt on the place', according to Dad. Mustering for shearing on one of those late March days that make you think that summer won't ever dissolve into autumn, Mum and Dad paused to discuss the best way to get the 'woolly brutes' home. They had 1,000 wethers in full wool to drive home, five miles in the heat. Mum was in the ute with Pud. Dad was on the bike. He decided to do one final check that they had got all the sheep, but told Mum to start pushing the mob homeward. 'Send Pud,' he told her.

Dad headed off, calm in the knowledge that the mob would be halfway home by the time he caught them up. Unfortunately, Pud wasn't about to let the mob move until the boss returned. This is where, he left them, and this is where they'd stay.

'Come behind, Pud,' came the casual instruction from the ute. Pud stayed put.

'Hind, Pud,' Mum yelled. No response. The door of the ute creaked open as Mum stepped out.

'Pud! Come behind,' was the command, this time the frustration evident in her voice. Mum had never been renowned for her patience, or her gentle temper—and the heat and flies, combined with a hard morning's bumping around the rough paddock after 'maggoty sheep' had done little to improve her mood.

'Come behind, you bloody useless mongrel.' Mum started to stride around the mob. Like the fine example of a working sheepdog that he was, Pud loped around the mob to cover the opposite side.

For the ensuing hour, Mum shouted, screamed, ran, swore, cursed and wheedled her way after Pudden, with no result.

Dad returned looking for the mob, to find his wife beside herself with rage, and Pud, cool as a cucumber, tail wagging and smiling at his master. The sheep had not moved an inch. Mum maintains to this day if she had had a rifle, Pud would have been an ex-working dog.

This is our farm dog Sally, a kelpie–huntaway cross. She was the best dog we've ever had, and we've had many over the years. Always loyal, and friendly to everyone. She liked a bit of attention and would do almost anything we asked her to do. She was an excellent sheepdog and a good companion. This shot of her is when we were getting her to play the part of the mascot on an old Mack truck in 2012. She loved this bit of fun and really took to it like she had seen exactly what the original looked like. Unfortunately Sally passed away in July 2013 after being with us for fifteen years.
Merv French, Northam, WA

These are our gorgeous four-legged friends! They always keep an eye on their Dad and make sure he's never far away. Here we are moving the tractors after hay carting and, as always, they've got one eye on his whereabouts. They're always always ready for work, whether it's at 5.30 am loading sheep for the sale yards or 1.30 pm on a dusty summer's day in the sheep yards, they're ready to help as soon as they hear the door handle turn. To describe these dogs as man's best friend is an understatement. They're always smiling and can always make the darkest of days bright. **Sarah Hodges, Baldry, NSW.**

Earning her keep
Joyce Chandler Ceduna, SA

This photograph is of our working cattle dog. Nugget works with dairy cattle, calves and beef cattle. He's a good jumper and likes to jump onto the round bales of hay. From his elevated position he barks and smiles at the people below. He is a friendly dog who likes people. **Ruth Timperon, Blumont, Tas**

We picked her up from the neighbours down the road. She was a small brown kelpie pup and we named her Brownie, for obvious reasons. She was a good all-round farm dog, who liked travelling on the front of the motorbike when needed for sheep work.

What was unusual about Brownie—and it is a story that still makes us laugh—is that she insisted on riding on top of the wheat bags being trucked from the farm to the silo. In those days harvesting involved bagging the wheat and driving it the long miles to the port where it was stacked ready for shipping to overseas markets.

There she would be, wind whistling through her hair as she enjoyed the view perched high on the bags. When we arrived at the weighbridge, no amount of calling would get Brownie off the load and she would inevitably be weighed in with the bagged wheat.

However, when weighing out after the wheat had been lumped off the truck, she could never be found—thereby always giving us a higher net weight and a few more shillings for our load. When we were ready to leave the port, this perverse creature would hop up into the cabin of the truck and sleep all the way home on the floor. It would be interesting to know how much extra she earned for us over the years.

A small black outlaw with an honest heart

Margaret Glendenning Everton, Vic

I am not sure where Dot came from. She just arrived. I was only a child and I welcomed her without hesitation into our family of animals and people.

Somehow, I gained the impression that she had been suddenly and desperately in need of a home, and had been passed from hand to hand in search of one. There was something about her previous owners moving away from the district in mysterious circumstances, and with great haste. Such details didn't trouble my curiosity for long—it was not until later years that I began to wonder about her life before she came to live with us.

A small, black kelpie with alert brown eyes, she was not young. Polite, but slightly reserved at our first encounter, she settled in easily with us, though she ignored the hunting dogs. Dot proved to be a good paddock dog, and useful in the yards. She never barked—no use ordering her to 'push up' and 'speak up'. Still, she managed to get her woolly charges right where she wanted them, without uttering a sound.

The hidden talents of our new helpmate did not become apparent for some time. One late afternoon my father stood watching a large mob of sheep stream through the gate past him, heading for the open paddock. One of the animals caught his eye as it leaped upward to canter off towards the hills.

'Should have had a look at that one,' he said as he stepped forward and pointed to the rapidly retreating wether.

I had been idly watching Dot where she sat behind the fence rails. I saw her galvanise into instant full speed, shooting out under Dad's arm like a little bolt of black lightning. In no time at all the indicated sheep was back almost at our feet, unhurt, but on its side and helpless. Dot held on firmly with absolutely no intention of letting go.

I watched her in action many times after this demonstration. We only had to quietly say 'That one' and point. She never failed to bring her quarry silently and quickly back to us. We used her to single out a 'killer' for the table or to capture an animal out of the mob that may have needed our treatment for fly strike.

A neighbour, watching her performance one day, laughed and slapped my father on the shoulder. 'Got yourself a duffer dog there, Jack!'

I didn't understand that remark. To me, a duffer was someone who unintentionally made errors, a bit of a bungler. Dot was no duffer—she didn't make mistakes. Her neat responses never wasted time or energy and I was sure she understood every word we said.

Time passed. Dot grew old and a little deaf. Like many aged dogs, she seemed to hear what she wanted to hear without any trouble. I was older, too. I now knew about 'duffer dogs'. I recalled how she would sit at dusk, tense, quivering, with some unknown excitement, staring at the moon rising over the distant hills. Was she remembering happenings of her past life, or was I just inventing them for her? I could well imagine the scene. The vehicle furtively hidden in trees by the fence, the hushed whispers and shadowy figures. The barely heard, low whistle. An elusive dark wraith silently dropping sheep one by one, standing over them until they were collected. Another farmer complaining angrily after finding a dozen sheep missing when next he tallied his mob.

Dot slipped her collar one night. I doubt she knew what hit her on the nearby road. We missed our little duffer dog, our small black outlaw with the honest heart, and I was not the only one who cried.

Australian cattle dogs don't suffer fools easily … but if and when they decide you're okay then you'll have a loyal friend for life. **Sally Harding, Albury, NSW**

Rover's rope

C C Cooper Jamestown, SA

Many years ago my father was killing a sheep for the home table with, as usual, his dog Rover watching his every move.

When Dad reached the stage where he was ready to pull the carcase up off the ground, the rope which he always used was just not there. For a moment he hesitated, then walked off to get a rope.

He had not walked many steps when he met Rover coming to him dragging a rope in his mouth. It wasn't the right one, but Rover had realised what was needed.

My son Ethan and his dog Awesome. They are very well-suited companions: both love the farm life, and both are very laid back. Inseparable, they often head out on little farm adventures together, neither returning without the other. Awesome loves to be in the shearing shed … if only to pose as the overseer. **Jade Norwood**; photo sent in by **Sharnie Mahar, Ceduna, SA**

Messiah of the lambs

Garth Outfield Wellington, NSW

We run about 4,000 sheep on 'Stockyard Creek', our property on the shores of Burrendong dam. The views of its waters from most of our paddocks are great but it's in winter, when the hills are cloaked in fog, that I find myself overawed by the beauty around me. On cold crisp mornings, shrouded in mist, I ride through mobs of lambing ewes to ensure that all are safe and to retrieve any lambs rejected by their mothers. Many a cold wet orphan lamb has been revived with a warm bottle of milk by the open fire in the homestead. And so to my dog tale.

As a young man I saw many funny incidents involving dogs, but I reckon that Sam, the whippet–beagle cross, one of the members of the rabbit pack, gave me the biggest laugh. Sam's position in the pack was semi-fast rank outsider in any chase, with very little chance of ever coming up with the prize money. He was a likeable dog, pure white with black patches stretching up over each eye to cover his large floppy ears. This description is important.

Mustering and lamb marking time had come around again—a time of year most of us sheep men don't much like. This particular year we were a bit late and the lambs were wild and large. As the bellowing ewes hung back, all trying to find their lost lambs in the mob, the lambs started to ring the edge of the mob, with more and more joining in the 'frisky' run. I knew we were in trouble. I had turned the surging tide back into the centre three times. Sheepdogs and motorcyclists were becoming frantic when strolling across the hill fair bang in front of the mob came Sam.

You can't imagine what I called him. Sam knew he was in trouble and turned for home. At the same time, however, the lambs broke and, seeing a pure white comrade (albeit with black floppy ears) making a beeline away from the mob, they followed.

Sam glanced back but was not impressed to find upward of 300 charging lambs bearing down on him and a further 400 screaming ewes coming after them. Sam changed into a higher gear and headed for home.

I was thinking murderous, unprintable, blasphemous thoughts about 'white rabbit dogs'. But being dimwitted as sometimes I am, I hadn't recognised heaven-sent assistance when I saw it.

Sam bolted for home. The lambs followed as though he was the anointed Messiah of all sheepdom. The faster Sam went, the faster the lambs went. He tried to lose them at the creek, but the leaders cleared it like Olympic long-jumpers. Sam stuck to the road like glue except for a smart circular move through a patch of scrub which he had learnt from chasing foxes. But, because the lambs were strung out through it, he ran into them wherever he turned. He soon dodged back to the road at even greater speed.

The gates had all been left open and Sam made full use of them—but still the lambs followed their leader, propping and bucking with glee. As we watched in astonishment from the rise where it all started, we could see Sam approaching the yards. The lambs were gaining on him. My mother looked up from the homestead garden and was aghast to see a line of 300 lambs heading for the yards with no ewes in sight. They were strung out far behind, all panting.

Finally, after being pursued for a mile, Sam hurdled the gate at the sheepyards and escaped to the safety of his kennel. All we had to do was pick up a few exhausted ewes along the way. When we finally reached the yards, my mother had already closed the gate.

This event happened about twenty years ago, but I can still see the tears of laughter rolling down my dad's cheeks. Sam probably had recurring nightmares.

Spud, a white border collie from Ouse in Tasmania, owned by Bernard McGlashan, showing his strength and power to walk up calmly, nose to nose with three Coopworth ewes. Not only is this strength used on the farm, but also as seen here in three-sheep trialling. **Louise Grant, Westbury, Tas**

Orders from on high

Natalie Broad Cue, WA

Bo, my seven-year-old huntaway, eyeing the sheep while drafting. My wife refuses to help in the yards because the of the yelling, but Bo is always willing to work and wag her tail after the odd cross word. Bo and I manage to do all the drafting and sheep work without the wife now. I'm not looking forward to the day when Bo is not around any more, as it's going to take a lot of sweet words and bribing to get my wife back into the yards.
**Peter Waterhouse,
Latham, WA**

Fred was a little, red, rough-coated kelpie dog belonging to Eric, my brother-in-law. He was top dog of the seven we had at the time, but very definitely a one-man dog who worshipped the ground Eric walked on.

During mustering time five years ago, Eric was flying the plane, and Jenny, the jilleroo who was working with us at the time, decided to take Fred because she had seen how useful he was. We have an 800,000-acre sheep station in the Murchison, so we cover a lot of miles, especially at mustering time.

Eric directed Jenny onto a large mob of toey sheep. They started to go in about ten different directions at once, so she screamed and signalled to Fred, 'get back there.' All he would do was run along next to the motorbike, waiting to jump on for a free ride. He wasn't going to work for her! According to Fred, he only had one master—and it definitely was not Jenny.

Eric flew over again and saw that Jenny was still having trouble trying to control her mob. Over the mustering radio attached to the front of the bike, he asked her what the matter was. She tried to explain her plight. The other musterers were too far away to come and assist, plus they had mobs of their own to control. The only option was for Fred to lift his game.

Jenny called Fred back to the bike and Eric whistled into his radio and told Fred to 'get back round there'. Fred shot off the back of the bike like a bullet and did what he knows best. Jenny stared in amazement at this dog who, after taking his orders from his boss in the air, had the mob under control in no time at all.

Heeling the runaway

Daphne Bannerman

Macleay River, NSW

When my elder daughter was born, we had a blue heeler dog. While being a very good dog with the cows, he was also very good with her.

From the day she came home from the hospital, the minute she cried, he would bark and alert me. I always knew when she was crying if I was outside. He was a perfect babysitter, circling the house so much that he wore a track around it.

When she learned to walk, he followed her everywhere, but the minute I called her and she started to run away, he would knock her over and wait until I got to her.

Exactly eight

Wally Karger Vale Park, SA

I sold some sheep to a chap at Kersbrook and he brought along a double-deck semi-trailer. I offered my dog Lassie to help load them, but he said his dog would do the job.

And my word she did. After the driver counted out eight sheep and put them in the first pen against the cabin and closed the gate, his almost-white border collie bitch loaded the bottom and top pens on her own—with exactly eight sheep in every one.

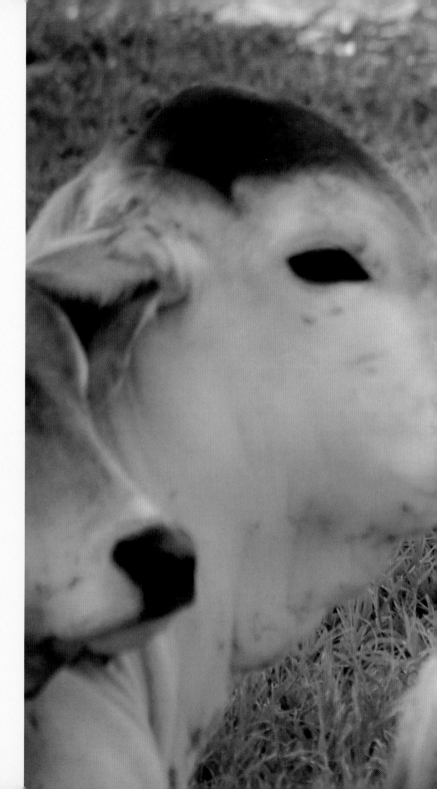

Border collie puppies start young! Brei, six weeks old, practising on the poddy calves.
Louise Stonehouse, Pentland, Qld

78

Hello–o–o, Dingo

Cavell Keevers Sandgate, NSW

Working dogs are the backbone of most farming enterprises producing meat and wool. Dogs can simplify many of the day-to-day tasks in stock husbandry. Their instincts have been honed over the years to match the requirements of farmers, from rounding up the stock to loading them in the truck. The range of genetic traits available to dog breeders is amazing, from herding abilities through to size and temperament. A working dog's focus in life is to work, and we are the lucky recipients to harness this talent. A good dog can save many hours of human labour—not to mention also giving companionship freely, along with the wag of a tail—and all a dog asks for is a feed and a warm kennel! **Ann James, Casterton, Vic**

Having lived in a forest area on the north coast of New South Wales where dingoes were plentiful, I have developed great respect for the intelligence of our native dog. Its cunning is extraordinary.

Our family has had several half-bred dingoes, but one stands out in my memory. We called him Dingo. He was the result of a furtive mating of my father's blue heeler bitch by a big red dingo which had forced its way into a locked slab barn.

Dingo, who was red like his father, was a wonderful household pet and a very intelligent farm working dog who seldom left my father's side. Because of this he frequently used to hear my father shouting 'Hello-o-o' to the neighbours when a telephone call came in for them. This was in the early days of telephones, and the neighbours had not yet installed one. The dog would sit by my father's feet and echo this call.

One day a friend living on a heavily timbered property nearby came to me very distressed, saying, 'Something seems to be wrong across the road from me. I can hear someone calling out "Hello-o-o" repeatedly, as if he needs help. I have searched the scrub and called out, but got no answer.'

When I told him that it was probably Dingo, he was most indignant, but had a laugh about it later.

After my father's death I lived by myself in the forest area. This half-bred dingo became very protective of me and would snarl and bark savagely to prevent any stranger from entering the front gate. I well remember the look of disbelief on people's faces when I told them to say 'Hello-o-o, Dingo' to be allowed inside. As soon as they did, however, the snarl would be replaced by a smile and a wave of the red tail. I must admit, though, that they always kept a close eye on the dog as he followed them up the garden path.

A total workaholic

Max Verco Marcollat, SA

Every now and again you get an outstanding dog, a champion. Joker was one of those.

In the 1930s, I worked on a property in the Flinders Ranges. Central Mount Stuart was on this place. The country was very steep and the ranges were terribly craggy. The scenery was magnificent, but, oh, it was very hard country to work. You were constantly up and down rocky mountains with lovely native pines on their slopes and creeks at their base.

Joker lived with me out on camp. It was only him and me. We became very close. He used to come inside the building but it was a pretty rough old place. It only had dirt floors. There were no beds in it, so I cut some pine logs and nailed a few bags between them to save me camping on the floor. It was my only little bit of luxury. In the really cold weather, old Joker used to sleep on my feet.

Now, when I was mustering in those ranges, I used to ride along on the top of the range. The idea was that I would chase the sheep off the top and down the steep slopes to the valleys on either side where it was easier travelling for the sheep and horses. About halfway down one side of the craggy range, I'd place a man and his horse, and another horseman down at the base. The bloke halfway down would pick up my sheep and push them down to the next bloke, who would collect them and drive them along the creek beds to the end of the range. On the other side, I needed only Joker to do the work of these two men on their horses. I only had to show him the job once, and ever after that he knew that he was the bottom man. He had so many more brains than any other dog. If there were sheep halfway down, he would go up and get them and take them along. When we got to the end of the range, he'd have his mob, and the other two fellows would have theirs.

When I left there, I got a job on a station in New South Wales. I went round by boat from Adelaide, and when I went in to get my ticket round to Sydney, I told the people in the office that I had a very good sheepdog and that I wanted to take him with me on the boat. They told me to put him in the care of the butcher. I told them I was very fond of this dog, that he was a mighty dog, and to tell the butcher to really look after him, or we would have an argument at the end of the trip. By that he had to make sure the dog had food, water, a bed, and didn't fall overboard, or I would deal with him. It only took three or four days to get around to Sydney. When I went to get Joker from the butcher, he was like a bloated toad! This butcher, he looked after him all right. I reckon he used to sling him a shoulder two or three times a day. Joker could hardly walk. It was a hell of a shock for a dog used to getting only a few scraps out of my saddlebag when we were out for a week at a time in that tough country.

When I got up to the station, because he was so good, I got all the best droving jobs. If I hadn't had a top dog, I would have got jobs like cleaning out the sheep manure from under the shearing shed and fencing.

Once, in 1932, I was bringing a mob down from New South Wales to Hallett in South Australia. We were on the road for about six weeks. Out in that back country, there were no fences.

My two working dogs on the veranda of our homestead in Collarenebri. Lucky (border collie) has a rest while Doc (kelpie) stays alert in the background, despite the mercury being in the mid 40s. **Braden Hamilton, Collarenebri, NSW**

You just let the mob spread. I was the youngest on the team, so while the others had a feed, I got the job of riding slowly around the mob to keep them more or less together. I only had to do that for two or three days, and then I just gave Joker a sign.

Every dinner time after that, he'd take over. I'd go into the camp with the men while we boiled our billy and had a bit of tucker. Joker would start one side and gradually work his way right around the mob, just easing a few in here or there that were heading out. It would take him almost twenty minutes to do the round. We used to time him! When he got opposite us he would look over at me and I'd just wave again, and he would start on his way back.

There wouldn't be many dogs you could teach to do this. Most would go around them if you sent them, but they'd push the sheep in on you, and have them milling all around the camp.

In those days there was no refrigeration, and in that country, it was as hot as hell. We had to salt all our meat, and when you were out on camp, you had salt meat and damper and hot plum jam. You didn't eat much. You couldn't. It was just too hot. You'd toss a bit to the old dog, and that's about all he had—a bit of salt meat. They were tough dogs but, like Joker, never happy unless they were working.

Bluey Warner

Mavis Taylor Uranquinty, NSW

Bluey Warner, as the name implies, was a warner. If any stranger seemed the least bit aggressive, the dog would stroll over and take his heel gently in his mouth. But he had even more sense than that.

One day, my two youngest girls went across to the neighbours' place to see their two mates. As with most children, they didn't use their heads. Away down to the creek they went to play in the water—a novelty as we hadn't had rain in ages. Typically, they thought they just had to get in and get wet. The creek was fairly deep where they were and flowed into two dams before careering on down through our place.

Fred went out to milk, but Bluey Warner, who always had the herd waiting for him at milking time, wasn't there. This was so unusual, because you could nearly set the time by the dog. So Fred smelt trouble.

'Where are the girls?' he asked.

I told him they were over at the neighbours' place.

'Bluey Warner hasn't brought the cows in,' he said. 'Let's go.'

We went next door and told them the dog had not brought the cows in. And so the search was on.

Down at the creek we were met by four bedraggled children and a muddy dog coming up the track. They had climbed down into the creek and couldn't get out. The power of the rushing, rising water had been pushing them toward the dams. They had been four very frightened children on the brink of a tragedy.

They had called out, hoping to make someone hear up at the house. We lived about a half-mile from the creek and although we hadn't heard their calls, Bluey Warner had.

According to the eldest child, he turned up on the bank and they tried to get him to go for help. Instead, he crouched down and grabbed the eldest girl by her clothes and started pulling. This was enough to enable her to get a foothold on firm ground and she scrambled out. She then lay down on the bank and pulled the other three out.

The children said Bluey Warner snarled and snapped at them. They couldn't believe his behaviour. We know dogs can't talk, but clearly they were getting a roasting from him, and a warning never to try playing in a swollen creek again.

My loyal companions. It was in the middle of our big drought. Temperatures were in the late 40s, there'd been no useful rain for five years, and we had to bring the cattle in for spraying. Smithy (the tail-ender) and the love of his life, Missy (the noser), worked hard at their tasks and went for a dip in the creek to cool off after we had the cattle penned. **Arthur Stafford, Toogoolawah, Qld**

He found his own mob

Bruce Mills Tumby Bay, SA

It was mustering time, and we were in thick mallee country, west of the Middleback Range. My mate and I set out from the homestead on the east side of the range. We were on horseback and accompanied by my mate, Spike. Our destination was an old caravan which had been placed in a small collecting paddock by a dam a few days earlier. It had been equipped for a week's mustering.

About three and a half miles from our destination, we saw a mob of sheep camped on the edge of a clearing, with very thick scrub behind them. The sheep saw us and stood up. Knowing that the scrub was very thick and hard to gallop through, we decided to send Spike around the sheep.

Now Spike, in spite of his faults, had a very good cast. Away he went, and we waited for ages for him to move the sheep, but nothing happened. The sheep started to drift off into the scrub. We decided that Spike must have put up a kangaroo (his main fault!) and left the sheep. After much scrub-bashing and many scratches we turned the sheep ourselves and, cursing the useless dog, took them to the camp.

We arrived there at sundown, and, after seeing to the horses' needs, set to getting something to eat for ourselves.

I was worried about my dog. I thought he must have been ripped open by an old scrubber kangaroo and was probably lying injured or dead somewhere. We were just about to climb into bed when we heard movements in the bushes outside. On investigating, we found the caravan ringed with sheep, held there by Spike.

No doubt in his original cast, he had found another mob of sheep further out and had followed us into camp with his own mob.

Spike had never been to this camp before and to get there had had to find and negotiate a narrow neck in the salt lake, a fact we checked out next morning. Needless to say Spike received much praise and a good feed, and I slept well.

Shallie, the faithful

Jim Hardy Penong, SA

It was just before shearing and Shallie, my six-year-old red kelpie bitch, and I had mustered up the wethers on the scrub block, 30 miles from the house.

We put them in a yard for the night before heading home. At 6.30 next morning Shallie and I left in the ute to bring the sheep back to the home block. When we arrived at the yards we found that the sheep had broken out, so I scouted around in the vehicle and found them on the edge of 3,000 acres of scrub. I let Shallie out to drive the sheep back to the yards through about one mile of scrub. While she was doing that, I went back to the yards to get a motorbike so I could help her.

On my way back to her, the wheel of the bike hit a tree root and I fell heavily. I landed on my back, onto a large stone. I couldn't move my body or legs — and realised my back was broken.

Shallie reached me after about half an hour. She drove the sheep around me, but sensed something was wrong so left the mob and came over to me. She licked my face and then lay down beside me. I dragged myself about 30 yards along a fence but couldn't go any further because the wire was cutting my hands.

So I just settled down to wait for the family to come looking for me. I knew it would be ages because they would probably think I had dropped into the pub on my way home, or something like that.

I wrote a note on a matchbox and hooked it onto Shallie's collar. I told her to go home, 30 miles away, but she wouldn't leave me. She just lay beside me all day from 9.30 in the morning until 9 o'clock at night, when finally a search party with a spotlight found me. The only way they could spot us was by picking up the shine of Shallie's eyes as she jumped up and down. An ambulance came and collected me, and Shallie was taken home.

Next morning, when my wife called Shallie, she wasn't there. She was found fifteen miles up the road on her way back to where she had been with me all day on the previous day.

While I was in hospital for three months learning to cope with life in a wheelchair, Shallie would not go near anyone, even for a pat. She must have been fretting. When I finally returned home, she went back to being her old self.

Since that accident, she retired from sheep work and spends all her time alongside my wheelchair.

Buddy is a border collie aged five. When he's not at work he loves lounging around. As he hardly ever leaves my side, I tried to get him to move out of the way, but being a border collie he can sometimes be stubborn. So what do you do when you want a picture of the sunset but the dog doesn't move? You just leave him in the picture. **Wayne Hunt, Forster, NSW**

As popular as a new governess

John Hawkes Yaraka, Qld

In 1985 at Mt Marlow station near Yaraka, Queensland, I was walking a mob of about 2,000 sheep down the Barcoo River when the overseer, Steven Gray, brought down a pup he had just got from Arno, the neighbouring property.

He dropped it on the ground to see if it would show any interest in the sheep. An hour later, four of us eventually caught it. In that time he had circumnavigated the mob a dozen times in an orderly fashion, never pursuing too hard or once cutting off a sheep.

I was very impressed and next week went over to Arno. After a carton of home brew, I eventually persuaded Billy Morton to part with the last of the litter, a black and tan kelpie dog. I named him Jess after Jesse Owens, the athlete.

As a contract musterer, I travel extensively with Jess. He is as popular as a new governess at every place we go. He is a natural backer, will unload trucks and swims rivers to get to sheep in a tight spot.

One day I was mustering at Diamond Downs for John Parkinson. I was in my Cessna 150 and my wife, Neen, was on the ground with Jess, John Parkinson, his daughter Kerry, and Tony Morley. They were all on motorbikes. We were mustering four paddocks as though they were one—20,000 acres in all—as the fences were shot. As it turned out, the main mob (about 1,500) ended up on one side of the fence, and little mobs of a dozen or more were scattered through the scrub all over the other paddocks.

One by one people were directed to other mobs until four stockmen were in one paddock putting together 500 stubborn sheep while Jess was in a paddock by himself with 1,500. He was, I could see from the air, also going through the broken-down fence at every sweep of the tail of the mob and working into the mob any that were getting through. With about two kilometres to go to the corner, everything looked pretty well under control, so I radioed the boss and told him I'd fly home.

He said, 'Well, I've only got a hundred or so here, and I can see Tony hasn't many. Who's with the main mob?'

'Jess has them in the next paddock,' I replied. 'He'll block them in the corner and wait for you there.'

And sure as eggs, that's what he did.

Someone later volunteered to give Jess his headset, so I could tell him what to do from the air.

'You hang onto your headset,' I said. 'Jess knows what to do.'

It's been a tough drought here in north-west New South Wales and feed is very hard to come by. My husband was asked to muster some feral goats off a nearby property and was taking Moss, a fawn and tan kelpie who is by far the best working dog I have seen. Moss loves his job, be it mustering sheep, cattle or goats, or moving my ducks.
Arlie McCumstie, Goodooga, NSW

A bit of a show-off

Max Nitschke Keith, SA

Most dogs work for just one master. If anyone else tries to reproduce the commands they know, or tries to give them a task, they usually react with disdain—and go off and lie under a tree. Sometimes, they'll just be confused and not understand what it is that another is trying to tell them to do. So it's an unusual dog that will work for absolutely anybody.

Enter Trixie, who was used by all the neighbours in the Marcollat district in the south-east of South Australia whenever they had something their own dogs couldn't handle. At lamb-marking time, she was particularly sought after. Lambs are difficult to control because they tend to run blindly in all directions. It takes a special kind of dog to keep calm with lambs and not rush them. So they called in Trixie.

She was good with everything. In fact she was a bit of a show-off. At shearing time, when all the sheep were penned up and she didn't have anything to do, she would come down to the house and work on the white rooster. Whether, because of his colour, she thought he needed shearing too, no-one knows. But she would separate him from the hens and nose him right up to the shearing shed, then inside the door—much to his displeasure. The old rooster would be cackling with annoyance and the shearers and everyone in the shed would laugh.

Trixie would also do her sheep work under remote control. I could stand on the front verandah and send her out to the far paddock to bring in a mob. She'd go out in the direction I pointed, then at a certain distance look back for further instructions. If she couldn't see me clearly, she'd stand up on her hind legs for a better view. If she still couldn't see my hand signals clearly, I'd use a long stick. Whichever side I was pointing to, she'd go until she found the mob and brought them right back in.

I also used to put her in charge of mobs of ewes and lambs that I was sending to market. They'd be in a paddock about two miles from the yards and are always really slow to move because lambs get separated from their mothers and the mothers fuss around. Anyway, at smoko time, I'd usually feel like a cuppa, so I'd leave Trixie to carry on alone. Whenever I got back to her, she'd still have every sheep and would be a good half mile closer to the yards. She would never leave any behind because she would only go the pace of the slowest sheep. Too many dogs will push them and make them scatter.

Trixie was a border collie, and I must have had her for thirteen or fourteen years.

I really missed her when she was gone. You only get about three good dogs in a lifetime.

I reckon those days were especially good for dogs. It was fairly wet here and you couldn't get out in a vehicle. If you wanted a mob of sheep brought in, you walked. While you walked, you could train a dog and the dog could hear everything you said. Since I've had motorbikes, I've had nowhere near as good dogs. Bikes are so noisy and we rush and tear around with the dogs on the back yapping and barking. I miss old Trix, and those days.

Rick the long-legged border collie seems to be dancing with his sheep in this photo. Rick came from Northern Ireland and made the long journey to Australia two years ago. **Kathy Gooch, Pearsondale, Vic**

This photograph was taken on 1 December 2013, at a working dog trial at Mia Mia in Victoria. The dog was moving sheep through a series of gates into another pen. He was brilliant!
Susan McBratney, Trentham, Vic

Old Bill

Gladys Maddison Macksville, NSW

Old Bill, a black and tan kelpie, was about sixteen years old at the time of this incident.

I was bringing in a flock of young ewes with their first lambs and it was close to dusk. The gate was awkwardly placed and Rover, an untrained puppy, was over-enthusiastic and separated one ewe from the flock. It careered down the paddock with Rover in full pursuit.

Meanwhile the ewes and lambs went quickly through the gateway with a little encouragement from Bill. I fastened the gate. Rover had returned, but when I looked around for Bill, he had disappeared, so I went off to look for the errant ewe.

It was nearly dark by now. I tried to get Rover to guide me to the ewe, but he didn't understand. The paddock was rough and boulder strewn, so it wasn't easy to find one missing ewe.

However, I heard a distant barking at intervals, then silence. I went down the gully in the direction of the barks. Rover left me and I followed him quickly, knowing he would lead me to Bill and, I hoped, the ewe.

When I reached the two dogs, there was the ewe up to her neck in a waterhole that was only her length in diameter. She couldn't get out but old Bill, at the side of the pool, was hanging onto her wool with his teeth, letting go, barking to attract my attention, and grabbing her again so she wouldn't sink.

It was quite an effort to haul her out as she was in full wool and waterlogged. After a short rest she went back up the hill to her baaing lamb.

It was all in a day's work for Bill. He retired a few years later as he was becoming deaf, but he lived to be 22 years old!

You silly mug

Arthur Finney Broadbeach Waters, Qld

It was early spring and as was usual I had risen at four-thirty. First thing was to send Patch, my ever-ready blue heeler, to round up the cows from the night paddock and drive them round to the yards for milking.

Meanwhile, I went back into the house for my usual early morning cuppa and piece of buttered bread. Coming down the back steps on my way to the yards, I looked over towards the night paddock. It was still shrouded in a light mist. In the half light I could vaguely discern the outline of what looked like a cow that Patch had missed.

'I'll give that dog the rounds of the kitchen when I get to him,' I thought as I walked over to the yards.

Patch had the herd penned when I got to the yards. He was just sitting at the gate waiting for me to shut them in.

When I scolded him for leaving one of the cows behind, he seemed quite perplexed, looking at me in the quizzical way he did when uncertain of my wishes. He baulked three or four times at going back to the night paddock. Ultimately, I had to really bully and threaten him before, with a very sulky manner, he trotted off to bring in the cow that I reckoned he had missed.

Had I stopped to think, I would have done a quick head count. This would have saved me considerable later embarrassment. I was certain I had seen a cow in the half light and morning fog.

There was no time to waste. Into the bails with the first six cows. Wash their udders and on with the machines. Get things moving, or I would be late for the milk carrier.

Then around the corner of the house fence appeared Patch, trailing old Darkie, my draughthorse, who was almost pensioned off. I had put him in the night paddock about a week earlier, and forgotten.

Patch slowly marched Darkie to the yard gate. He then sat on his haunches and looked across at me with an expression on his face which seemed to say, 'There you are, you silly old mug, try and milk that one.'

Yarding time, last job of the day. Lindy, my cream kelpie, works hard to keep the cheeky cattle in line. Whether it's walking cattle in, yarding up, feeding horses, swimming in the dam, doing a water run, or just lying around on the lawn, Lindy is always there to help me. She's tough, determined, strong and happy. That's my working dog Lindy.
**Kristen Ayliffe,
Longreach, Qld**

The bull-rider's debut

Errol Munt Toowoomba, Qld

This story happened some fifteen years ago and involved Gundy, a cattle dog I had been given as a pup by my uncle, Mr Norm Ehrlich.

I was on horseback and Gundy and I were trying to shift a Droughtmaster bull across the highway to the yards on the other side. We almost had him enclosed in the yard when he decided to break away and head back across the highway, which was about 250 metres away. The determined bull gathered speed and took no notice of either the horse or Gundy as we tried to block him.

When he reached the first road fence he leapt across the grid and over the highway and then smashed through a piping gate on the other side. By then I suppose he thought he was home and safe. This was not the case as Gundy and I were in hot pursuit. The language from me was 'blue' with rage, and Gundy was heeling him every step he took. By the time I opened the gate at the first fence and got across the highway, I could see the bull heading for the supposed safety of a dam. After a brisk

gallop to catch Gundy and the bull, I arrived to see the bull make a leap into the dam. Gundy duly followed.

In the next twenty seconds I changed from being extremely angry to laughing so much that I couldn't sit straight on the horse. Imagine seeing your dog swim up alongside a bull, climb upon his shoulders, stand there on all fours, and bite the bull on the back of the neck. A bull-riding dog—I hadn't seen that before.

Deciding the water was no longer the best place to be, the bull swam to the edge of the dam, with the dog still aboard. Then he climbed up the bank and stopped some three metres away from the water. At this stage, Gundy jumped off. He had ridden his eight seconds and got top points from the judge!

If only dogs could talk—in between eyeing off the bull, he would occasionally look back across the dam at me with a pleased look upon his face that seemed to say, 'I got him for you.' After a minute or two's rest so we could all regain our composure, the bull was willing to be driven anywhere without resentment.

Kendall River Station, Cape York, North Queensland. Border collies Ranger and Ruby working a mob of cows in the old cattle yards. My husband Les and I live and work on this cattle station for six months of the year (the dry season). This will be our sixth year; we take our own working dogs, about twenty in total, plus horses and quad bikes. Our dogs are an important part of our team—we simply could not get our jobs done without them. We've become a close team; basically, we live, sleep, eat and work together. **Simone Barton, Falls Creek, NSW**

A leaner Christmas without Lena

Christine Stratton Strathalbyn, SA

Red and Boots are two keen dogs with plenty of go, and if the boss calls they come. We love all our kelpies, and I have the best time photographing them in action. My passion for photography and our working dogs makes for the best frozen-in-time memories. **Arlie McCumstie, Goodooga, NSW**

In September 1978 we bought two dozen day-old turkeys to fatten and sell to help bring in some cash for Christmas. It had been a lean year for us. We put our two working collies, Lena and Sonny, on guard over the turkeys to ensure their safety.

At 11.30 one late November night, about two weeks before the turkeys were ready to kill and dress, we heard a terrible squawking coming from the barn where they were kept. We had thought they would be safe in the well-protected cage we had made. The dogs had been asleep on the old settee outside the back door. They took off, barking. As they ran toward the turkey cage they were met by a large fox with one of the biggest turkeys in its mouth.

The fox raced through the fence and into the paddock, with the dogs in full pursuit. We could do nothing but listen to the dogs barking as they chased the fox toward the dam. In the moonlight we could see the dogs circling the top of the dam wall and the fox swimming for its life. The dogs refused to let it leave the water and we found next morning that it did eventually drown.

'Well, there goes our Christmas dinner,' I said to my husband. We had taken orders for all but one turkey, which was to have been ours, so it looked like we would have to eat chicken.

Just then I felt something warm against my leg. There were the dogs looking very pleased with themselves, tails wagging like windmills, as Lena dropped the large white turkey at my feet.

That Christmas, no turkey ever tasted better. But I did swear the kids to secrecy until after the guests had eaten, even though I think the bird must have died of fright. There wasn't a mark on it when I dressed it.

Nacooma Gus: a legend in his own lifetime

Lyndon Cooper Kingston SE, SA

Over all the years I have been breeding and training working dogs, I have always found the true, all-round working dog the most fascinating and intelligent. He's the dog that can muster a paddock on his own, drive a mob of sheep to yards or homestead and also work in the yards when the mob has been yarded.

These dogs think for themselves. They seem to be able to work out where the stock has to go and they rarely get into trouble doing their work. Although I have great respect for a good yard dog, the all-rounder is the type of dog I enjoy breeding and working the most.

Nacooma Gus, my kelpie dog, a son of Bullenbong Mate, never ceases to amaze me with the level of intelligence he has. I remember one particular time a couple of years ago when I walked out from the homestead with Gus just on dusk. I cast him around a 60-acre paddock covered in thistles and dock to pick up a mob of 300 wethers that I had put in there a couple of days before in order to be drenched.

After about fifteen minutes, Gus returned without any sheep. I gave him some harsh words of advice and sent him out again to have another look. This time twenty minutes went by, but still no sheep and also no Gus. And it was getting quite dark. I returned home to collect the utility to look for the missing sheep and dog.

After driving around the paddock, I failed to find the sheep myself, so I headed for the gate into the next paddock which led into a laneway into the cattle yards. Much to my amazement, Gus and the 300 sheep were coming from the next 60-acre paddock into the laneway and out onto the track heading for home. Somehow the gate had been left open and the wethers had found their way into the next paddock.

Gus, obviously not being able to find any sheep in the first 60-acres, went through the fence and mustered the next paddock, found the sheep and knew where to take them to get them on the track for home.

At shearing time at our place there is always a lot of talk about dogs, some funny, some serious, but rarely does a shearer have to wait for sheep.

One year we had a new rouseabout. He was fascinated with the dogs and the way they would cast out into the hills, muster a mob of sheep and bring them into the yards while we were working in the shed. Only on the very odd occasion would they leave one behind.

At about 11 am on the second-last day of shearing, the weather was looking rather threatening and one of the shearers suggested we bring the last mob in. As I was busy wool classing, I took Gus out into the paddock and cast him out over the

This is my kelpie, Devil, at eighteen months. I got Devil as a tiny pup for free; every other pup in the litter had gone, as they'd all been carefully selected. I had no idea about working dogs or how to train them but couldn't let him be a reject, and so he came home with me. I was working on a place with around 30,000 sheep, and as a pup he'd just run straight into the middle of the mob and bark, splitting the mob. All the guys at work would laugh, but we were determined not to give up. And then a light switched on! I was feeding sheep with a trailer and they just wouldn't come, so I let Devil go and he ran up that huge hill and brought every girl to me! Later that week we were drenching without the boss's good dogs, and drenching in a loose race is a pain. I sent Devil and, lo and behold, away he went! From that moment on he backed, and on my very last day I was packing the races while the boys drenched. He's my best mate, and together we proved we could do it. **Grace Hambling, Mudgee, NSW**

bracken-covered hills, left him to it and returned to the shed to go on classing wool.

After about 30 minutes, much to the amazement of our bewildered rouseabout, over the hill and into the yards came this mob of sheep.

During lunch it started to rain, so we pushed these sheep into the shed. It was chock-a-block full. You couldn't fit another sheep in, but we felt very pleased with ourselves as it rained all day.

As we walked from the shed after knock-off time, the rouseabout spotted approximately twenty sheep up on top of one of the hills. He looked at me and said, 'What are those sheep up on the hill there, Coop? Gus never leaves any behind, eh?'

Thinking very quickly, I replied, 'Well, he knew they wouldn't fit in the shed, so he left those few behind.'

Well, I can tell you that rouseabout was the best publicity officer I could ever have employed because various versions of this true story circulated the local hotels for some time.

I know a dog may not be that smart, but for a dog that has won four State Farm and Yard Dog Championships, been in 56 finals and won 24 of them, represented South Australia in the National Titles four times being placed as high as third, as well as learning tricks like climbing ladders and walking backwards, I reckon he's capable of almost anything.

Birth on the job

Joyce Shiner Albany, WA

Sissy was a young red kelpie who was supposed to be chained up at shearing time, but this time somebody forgot. She was close to having pups and there were other dogs to do the work, so it was thought best that she was rested.

From the cookhouse window, I saw her drinking at the bowl under the tap, then she disappeared. Hearing a puppy yelping I went to investigate and found a pup in her bed. Several times she came back for a drink, each time leaving a pup or two. Then she would race back to the shed again.

At lunchtime we compared notes and discovered that Sissy had worked in the sheep yards all morning, returning to the house between jobs ostensibly for a drink.

The shearers were amazed to see her litter of newly born puppies, and she hadn't even missed a beat in the shed.

104

This is Dusty from Ashmar in Gloucester, New South Wales, having some time out behind the tractor wheels. If she's having a rest, so is everyone else. Dusty is exhibiting that wonderful ability that dogs have to be able to sleep anywhere at anytime. But she'd be up in an instant if there was the slightest hint of any work or any fun or if she felt there was a chicken that needed to be reminded to stay out of the shed. **Simon Holland, Springwood, NSW**

A huge vocabulary

Greg Walcott Horsham, Vic

I am one of the fortunate sheepdog owners to have been lucky enough to have owned the 'freak' dog whose intelligence was simply outstanding and quite unbelievable. I have owned several good or very good sheepdogs, but Whisky was extraordinary.

He was largely a self-taught dog. I trained him with the basics as a pup but rarely had to teach much else as he simply picked up things or worked things out for himself. His powers of reasoning and comprehension often amazed me.

His vocabulary was huge. I once read in a national daily newspaper that dogs could not learn more than twenty words, but simply reacted to tone of voice. As a result I wrote down in excess of 400 words in Whisky's vocabulary and quite often tested the tone of voice theory by including, in a conversation with someone, a simple order to Whisky in the same tone that I was using. He would invariably stir from his half sleep and do as suggested.

I was able to teach him many names—of people, pets, sheds, vehicles and so on. This was often very handy as I quite often used him to run messages to people. I would tie a note in a rag to his collar and send him off in search of a particular person—and he always found them.

One day I was having trouble drafting ewes. Whisky and I always drafted by ourselves with little or no trouble. This day, however, was very hot—the sheep were not running, the dog had his tongue out and I was getting hot under the collar. In desperation I decided to change the pens around to try to make things easier. In the meantime I told Whisky to 'Go and get a drink. Go to the dam and have a drink'—which he was only too pleased to do.

When I had sorted things out in the shed I called Whisky to start drafting again. There was no sign of him. I was really starting to get annoyed. I looked out of the shed to see Dad driving up from the house, which was about one kilometre away. He arrived looking very concerned and with Whisky on the front seat.

Whisky had knocked on the kitchen door demanding entry. When Mum opened it he marched straight past and up to the kitchen table. No sign of Dad so back past Mum, out through the lounge and up through the front room to where Dad was working at his desk. With a demanding couple of barks and an anxious look he about-turned and marched out with Mum and Dad watching in utter surprise and bewilderment. Thinking the worst, Dad followed him out to the car and promptly drove up to the shed to see what was wrong.

To this day I do not know if Whisky mistook 'dam' for 'Dad' or simply took it on himself to go and seek Dad's assistance with the drafting. Mum and Dad couldn't believe the assertive way he got his message across.

The dam's getting low. **Rod Marriage, Builyan, Qld**

107

Tina the nearly retired matron hangs back exhausted, while Jill the young pup enthusiastically works on with Tash the expert at her side, after a long day in the yards pushing up ewes. The three girls work together to get the job done, and never miss a beat. Great work ethic, determination, team work and a passion for success make these workers invaluable when getting a job done. The girls can easily push up 1,500 ewes in a day, with only a few whistles as commands. **Tom Ellis, Mt Gambier, SA**

Backing the blockage

Frank Bawden Tumby Bay, SA

Friend, sharefarmer and shearer Andrew Mills comes from a family of noted kelpie breeders, owners and trainers. Accordingly, he has a particularly good dog called Boy.

During shearing we were filling the shed from outside when the sheep baulked in one of the catching pens. Andrew sent Boy up onto the backs of the wethers, up the ramp and into the shed to look for the blockage.

My brother Bernie, who is big and hairy, was the shed hand. Unbeknown to us, he was bending down, nailing the grating in the catching pen into place.

Boy, true to form, darted over the backs of the sheep and landed with a big 'woof' right on Bernie's broad back. It's still debatable today who got the bigger shock. Bernie leapt into the air with shouted obscenities, while Boy must have suffered a good deal from shock also.

We spectators had considerable difficulty controlling our mirth. Needless to say, Bernie was at a loss to see what was so funny.

Why get wet?

Jack Rossiter Bellbrook, NSW

We live on the wrong side of the river in flood time, and on one occasion we had a power failure. It was necessary for a couple of county council men to be transported by boat to attend to repairs.

On arriving at the river bank, the two men and a dog waited for us to pick them up. The dog was the first in the boat. When we reached our side, the dog was first out.

That afternoon when we arrived at the river to transport the men back, there was the dog, sitting on the bank waiting to get across. He was first into the boat again.

As the men left the boat we mentioned their dog. They assured us it was not theirs and that they had never seen it before. When talking about the incident some days later, we found that the dog had come from about three miles away and had been visiting a lady friend on our side of the river.

Now a dog would be just too silly if he swam a flooded river twice when there was a boat service running to a suitable timetable, wouldn't he? So there he was, home and dry, after a pleasant day's dalliance—and he went back to doing his cattle work the next day.

The strange part about it was that the dog, from all accounts, had never been in a boat before.

110

Summer fun. **Robin Kissel, Hamilton, Vic**

The eye of the storm

Syd Nosworthy Lucindale, SA

When Ray Nosworthy set out to muster a remote property, he followed a well-established routine. He rode to the mustering hut, dropped some food and went on with his kelpie bitch, Brownie, to muster the sheep.

Having scoured the big paddock, he started the mob towards the hut. The routine was to place the mob in a section of fenced laneway, string wire across the mouth and spend the night in the hut ready to resume the journey next morning.

All had gone smoothly—until mid-afternoon. Brownie gave the first indication of trouble. Like many dogs, she was afraid of storms and Ray noticed she was tending to abandon her normal role of trotting slowly at the rear of the mob. While still keeping the sheep headed in the right direction, she kept returning to be near Ray's horse.

Before long the skies darkened and rolling thunder could be heard. Lightning and thunder were upsetting the dog, but with the hut in sight, Ray thought he would get the mob safely into the lane.

However, in the premature darkness rain began to fall. And how it rained. Great gusts of water cascading down reduced visibility to practically nothing. In the frequent lightning flashes, Ray saw that the sheep had broken and scattered. He could not see the dog and his calls were drowned in the wild rolls of thunder and the drumming of the pelting rain.

Abandoning the sheep, he rode to the hut expecting to find Brownie already cowering there. She wasn't. He turned his horse loose, lit the old lantern in the hut and called. There was no response. Leaving the lantern in the doorway to attract the dog's attention, he lit a roaring fire, stripped off his sodden clothes and strung them up to dry. After a meal, he still could not attract Brownie, so he reluctantly gave up and climbed into the bunk. The storm was still raging and the rain was unceasing. He was up at first light. The storm had passed but in its wake great sheets of water lay across the flat landscape.

Saddling his horse, Ray was surprised to see knots of sheep on high ground in the lane. A subsequent count amazingly revealed they were all there. As he neared the mouth of the lane, there was Brownie, half submerged in water, guarding the entrance to the lane.

Ray could only marvel, firstly at her skill in getting the sheep into the lane, and the amazing devotion to her task demonstrated by spending the night in conditions she found completely terrifying. When he reached her, she could scarcely move. Shivering and stiff, she had obviously remained at her post for hours. Knowing the sheep were not likely to escape through the water, Ray picked up the dog and carried her on the saddle to the hut.

Brownie was put in front of the fire to thaw out. She ate a few scraps and after a while appeared to be ready to work. The rest of the journey was across high ground and the sheep would be in their paddock by about midday.

It was soon obvious that Brownie was ill. Ray put her up in front of him on the saddle until they reached home, where he bedded her down. After patient nursing, she recovered but her lungs had suffered some damage. For the rest of her life, she wheezed and coughed with almost every movement. Although she learnt to canter for short distances, Ray realised she would never be able to work in the paddocks again. He put her into retirement but she wasn't happy.

However, Brownie was in luck. Ray's brother, Frank, suffered from a chronic heart condition that restricted him to walking pace only. He and Brownie fitted their lives together. She could yard the killers from a small paddock and she soon learnt to bring the cows in for milking twice a day.

Henry, in the back of the ute after a hard day working, looking unhappy about the drought. **Emerson Ross, Bundook, NSW**

Smoko time for Jade. Working in the shearing shed during the summer heat means a long, hot and tough day. Some sheds are lucky enough to have huge fans blowing on the shearers, and when the rousabouts have a quick free moment they duck in front of it to cool off. Spare a thought for the shed dogs, barking and pushing up sheep all day—it's extremely hot and hard work squeezing in among all those woolly sheep. When smoko time comes, these little legends dart straight out of the shed and head for the nearest troughs. After a quick cool off they are ready and eager to jump straight back in there to help us, in even the hottest conditions. **Sam Sullivan, Coonabarabran, NSW**

Working mother

V J Mengler Tenterden, WA

Tootsie was heavy with pups which, unfortunately for her, decided to appear just as shearing began. As everyone knows, sheepdogs are required to work very hard at shearing time, but with Tootsie facing motherhood, and then actually becoming a mother, she was put on 'maternity leave'.

For a few days she and the puppies were shut in their netted-in pen with kennel, food and water available. The puppies spent most of the time feeding or sleeping. However, this did not suit Tootsie. She heard the sheep and the men working in the yards, so on the first day her pen was opened for her to have a run, Tootsie worked out her own plan.

I was cooking in the kitchen but when I went to the back door I found that Tootsie had carried each pup about fifteen metres and placed it carefully on the back doorstep for me to babysit. She had already sped off to the shearing shed.

I put the pups back in the kennel, close together for warmth. As soon as lunchtime came, Tootsie dashed into her kennel, fed her brood, drank lots of water and was ready to go back with the men after lunch to work. She did the same at afternoon tea time and the routine continued for the rest of the shearing.

Sorting them out

Roy Postle Pittsworth, Qld

I was droving about 200 cattle from Toowoomba to Pittsworth when this event happened.

At a little place called Broxburn there is a watering point for travelling stock. The property either side of the stock route was owned by the Day brothers, who had a dairy and milked 45 to 50 cows. When I topped the rise, I saw that their dairy cows were on their way to the yards. However, two of my cows which had already had a drink were wandering off to join them.

I told Spot to get around them but they were in with the milkers before he could head them off. Without telling him to do anything else, I watched him go through the mob, find one cow and bring her out. Once clear of the milkers, a couple of good bites and she was on her way back where she belonged. Back he went again, and sure enough he did the same with the other cow.

While all this was going on, I was at least a quarter mile away, but the Day brothers were on the yard rails watching.

When I caught up to move the strays on, they called me over. They said if they had not seen what Spot had done they would never have believed it. And with a bit of a grin they asked if I would sell him. What would you think?

Michael Grant, with Fleetwood Queen at his feet—members of the Australian team competing with New Zealand in 2014—and Nitro, a border collie with a touch of kelpie, droving over 2,700 merino wethers along the Interlaken Road in the highlands of Tasmania. The drove was over a distance of 65 kilometres, took a day to muster and three days to drove and involved a team of five trial competitors of the Tasmanian Working Sheepdog Association. **Louise Grant, Westbury, Tas**

116

Good all-round

Wally Karger Vale Park, SA

Thanks, a young border collie pup born on the Brinkworth cattle drive, where 18,000 head of cattle were walked 2,000 kilometres, from Northern Queensland to Hay, New South Wales. The pup and its offsider, Please, showed a lot of early potential, shadowing the boss's every footstep when he was around the camp. When the boss stopped each day, Thanks and Please parked themselves right at his boots and waited for his return. Many pups were born on the drove. The drovers kept some and others were sold or traded along the stock route.
Alice Mabin, Roma, Qld

This is a true story of the life of a pup. We lived on a farm in the Adelaide Hills, running about 200 sheep, three cows, seventy chooks and ten geese. We trained Lassie from a six-week-old pup. Obedience was important, so she learned to sit and come at once. She also learned to pick up small articles and to put them into our hands, or in a bucket, or on a chair, wherever we told her to put them. We always gave her a small crumb or cornflake as reward.

Before she was six months old, she was able to bring me a pair of pliers, a screwdriver or a box of matches. She could even bring them out to where we were working in the paddock. Later, she learned to bring some sheep shears so we could treat fly-struck sheep.

In 1955, a bushfire burnt us out and we were broke. Lassie had become a sheepdog which we could lend to our neighbours. Our own sheepyards had been destroyed in the fire.

I had to go to work off the farm and Lassie would lie with no interest in sheep until 6 o'clock on Saturday morning. Then she would be at the door and I'd just say 'Fetch the sheep in' and after I had lit the fire and had breakfast, the sheep would be waiting at the gate to go into the neighbour's yards. She was both a yard dog and paddock dog and rarely left a sheep behind, even in the rough hills or scrub.

She was good with the geese too. If they wandered, my wife just had to say, 'Lass, the geese are on the road'. Very slowly, the geese would then be driven back to the dam where Lassie would watch them for an hour, sometimes not even allowing them out of the water.

Our neighbour, Murray, had Dorset Horn cross sheep and we had black-faced Suffolk rams. Murray's lambs always seemed to crawl under the fence and would join up with our black-faced ones. We always tried to drive them out before they got boxed up.

One Sunday, Murray phoned and told us to watch Lassie, who was over on the hill. There she was, very slowly, walking between fourteen big weaner lambs of Murray's and our mob. While the lambs were feeding, she worked them gently towards the fence. Then she put them through the hole and moved them up into Murray's yard, where she lay and watched them with her head on her paws.

One of her last chores, at the age of fourteen, was particularly memorable. We were irrigating from the River Murray. I had left my rubber boots down in the lucerne where the sprinklers were.

I was tired and weary, so I said, 'Fetch my rubber boots, Lass'. The poor old girl loped down to the lucerne, and after ten minutes appeared with one boot.

I repeated the order and she brought the other to the door. By this time, it was almost dark, but there were my boots.

Sandsoap

Ron Kerr Borroloola, NT

Forty years ago, I was tailing a mob of bullocks a few miles north of Bourke, New South Wales, along the Darling River at Mays Bend.

The bullocks had come from Nockatunga Station on the Wilson River, south-west Queensland. There were 1,250 head and after droving them for months from Nockatunga, they were well handled and the grass along the Darling was knee-high and green. We were waiting for the Bourke Meatworks to have enough room in the yard to take them.

It was a drover's dream tailing bullocks on tall green grass alongside clear running river water, compared to the country we had come over, with raw sand, dust, flies and scrub.

There were five of us in the camp—a horse-tailer, cook and three of us with the cattle, all taking turns to watch the cattle at night on open, soft ground free from gullies, logs or stumps. The spot for night camp was mostly picked by the cook and horse-tailer—a place where the night watchman had a chance to go with the lead of the cattle if they jumped. This mob had done plenty of that for the first week out of Nockatunga.

But now they were like milking cows and could be handled by one man. That's why that day I was on my own with the bullocks. It was my turn to tail the cattle.

I left the night camp at daybreak, with my corned beef and damper in the saddlebag and a quart pot on the other side of the saddle as I wouldn't be back to the camp until it was time to bed down the bullocks at dark that evening.

That night I wouldn't have to take a night watch and I was looking forward to a good night's sleep as everyone else in the camp would be sleeping most of that day. It was about dinnertime or midday when the cattle camped along the hollow in the river bed, so I put the quart pot on to boil.

When the horse, tied to the tree, started moving about, snorting now and then, I walked over to check if there were ants about, or whatever else might be upsetting it.

About twenty yards from the horse was a black and tan pup about two months old, and that poor I thought he'd have to stand twice before making a shadow. I felt like getting a good, strong stick and putting him out of his misery. He had big, sad eyes and wasn't frightened to look me in the eye with both of them. I tried to pat him, but he got up and moved about ten feet away. I tried again. He moved away again. I said, 'OK, you independent bastard. I've got a quart pot boiling away and I've got no use for a dog, as we've never had dogs in the camp.' I went back to making the tea.

Getting my corned beef and damper out of my saddlebag, I'd just sat down when I heard something behind me. Looking around, there was the pup with his big, sad eyes sitting under the shade near the horse. I thought, 'I'll win this dog over to my way of thinking.'

Breaking off some corned beef, I walked over to him, getting on the upwind side so he could smell the beef. It was no go. He could smell the meat all right. I could see his nose twitching, but he wouldn't come to me or let me touch him. It was just those big, goggle eyes that said nothing.

I threw the meat towards him. It hit the ground about six inches in front of his nose. I think it was still moving when it disappeared and I saw the lump snaking down the pup's throat. There was not even a wag of the tail. Just those big glassy eyes looking at me, or at something above my head.

I had finished eating as much corned beef as I wanted and still had plenty left over. From habit I always carry more corned beef than I need in case there is trouble with the cattle. You may miss a mealtime and beef was not short in this camp.

So, going to my horse to check out the cattle, I emptied what leftover food I had not far from the dog—who never made a move towards the meat. Riding away, I looked back. The pup was eating, so I left him to it and rode around the bullocks.

Half an hour later I was sitting on my horse under some shade when the horse tried to get a look behind him. I turned around and there was Big Eyes sitting under a tree twenty yards away. This went on every time I moved. The pup moved like he was some sort of tail-light.

About 3 o'clock the bullocks were on their feet starting to feed. I was kept busy working them out of the river, making them feed out over the river flats towards the camp. It was near sundown when I looked to see if the pup had followed. Sure enough, there he was, even though his eyes looked the biggest part of him.

Just on dark the horse-taller came out and gave me a hand to put the cattle on camp as he could then take my horse out to the others and hobble him, and bring back another night horse. With the cattle bedded down, I picked up my swag and took it over near where the night horses were tied up. Although I wasn't watching that night, I had to be up and on a horse if the cattle jumped.

The horse-tailer came up with the last night horse and asked where the bony, big-eyed pup came from. I told him he'd been following me at a distance all day along the river and I didn't want to chase him away as he might run into the bullocks and spook them. And as he was over near my swag I'd try to catch him and tie him up that night in case he put the cattle on their wheels.

The horse-tailer said, 'If you can fatten him you might see that he has a bit of breeding in him.' I said the breeding might be a long way in and the way he eats beef we might need the whole

mob to fatten him. But the horse-tailer said, 'He's a black and tan kelpie and could be close to purebred, and they don't bark much unless they're made to bark.'

That night when I went to my swag with a piece of fresh cooked corned beef, I was going to try to catch Big Eyes and tie him up with one of my swag straps. I started feeding him little bits of meat at a time. Each piece was gulped down but I still couldn't get a hand on him. At last I gave him all the meat. The way his gut came out you could see where the beef was.

A few days later, we moved off with the bullocks to the meat-works yards. There our long trip from Nockatunga finished and Big Eyes was there twenty yards behind me all the time.

From there, I looked up my brother, Frank, who was camped with his droving plant at North Bourke. Me and Big Eyes camped with Frank for a week or so, then a mate of mine came along looking for someone to go with him up on the Culgoa River towards the Queensland border, mustering sheep for shearing.

So next day, me and Big Eyes left for Kennibree Station, walking a plant of horses. Big Eyes wouldn't get up under the wagonette with the other dogs, so he followed me behind the horses for the 40 miles. By now, he was in my shadow all the time and I could put my hand on him. But he never wagged his tail. He just lay down and looked at me like I was stupid.

My mate Wally Smith said, 'He's a one-man dog if ever I saw one and if you just give him time, he'll make a worker and a good one at that. But you want to call him a name, and one that someone can't pick if you lose him. Big Eyes is too close to his looks.'

A few days later, we were washing our clothes down at the creek and Wally said, 'Have you worked out a name for the dog yet.'

I said I'd tried every dog's name I know and there was still no reaction. As I had a cake of sandsoap in my hand for washing, I said I might as well call him Sandsoap. The dog stood up and wagged his tail for the first time. Smithy said, 'That's close to his name. Call him Sandy.'

The reaction was now from the ears and tail.

Smithy said, 'Make it Sandsoap. It's harder for someone else to think of.'

So, Sandsoap it was. I now had a dog with a name and one I could pat, tie up and which had meat over his ribs.

For the next two days of mustering sheep, Sandsoap never got any more than ten feet from my horse, but he jumped up and down when Wally's dog went around the sheep.

Wally rode around the mob saying to me, 'Has Sandsoap taken any interest yet.'

I said, 'He goes ten feet from the horse and I go the rest. Not sure he'll be a sheepdog.'

Next morning, we were taking shorn sheep back to a paddock. I said to Wally, 'I'll tie this Soap dog up as he might cause trouble.'

Wally said, 'No. Bring him along. These shorn sheep're hungry and they'll take some holding until we get out onto some grass country.'

There was a small holding paddock near the shearing shed with about 1,000 shorn sheep, all snow white. Wally said for me to go down and open the gate and try to steady the lead of the sheep when they went through.

I opened the gate and out came the sheep. Now to steady the lead.

There was no lead. They were all round the horse, under the horse's belly and I was trying to get the horse to the outside. I looked for Sandsoap. Was he still in the middle under the sheep? I noticed that Wally's dogs must have blocked the lead as the sheep were starting to turn back.

Getting to the front of the mob, I saw Sandsoap doing about 30 miles an hour right across and just under the noses of the sheep. To give him moral support, I yelled, 'Stick it into 'em, Sandsoap.'

That sent him mad. He went around the lead and down the other wing. About 40 yards down the wing, he turned and came back, bringing the other point of the wing around and across the lead. I got out of his way as the lead came bolting around the

rest of the mob. I sat there on my horse and couldn't see a thing. There was a red cloud of dust 50 feet in the air.

Wally came around the other side of the mob covered in red dust, saying, 'That dog's starting to work.'

I said, 'He's gone mad and deaf. I can't call him back.'

'Don't try,' said Wally. 'He's ringing them back onto the fence and will stop ringing soon.' Sure enough, the dust was lifting as the sheep pulled up. Out of the dust came Sandsoap, his tongue almost on the ground and the goggle eyes were like fire. Watching the sheep, he almost ran into us before he saw us.

Wally said, 'I'll bet anything he's a born lead dog, a dog that wants to work on his own. Catch him, and hold him until I bring the tail up. Let the lead go for a while, then we'll give him the lead to work.'

By now, we were coming into grass country and the sheep were settling down, but still moving and spreading. I let Sandsoap go. His tongue was still hanging out, but he trotted across the tail of the mob, stopped once, looked back, then loped off up the wing. Later we could see him trotting back and forth across the lead.

Shearing cut out three weeks later and I stayed behind to work as overseer for the next three years. Sandsoap started as a jackeroo pup and went on to be head stock dog.

I saved some money, bought a truck and went back droving cattle. Sandsoap became well known around the drovers' camps.

I was taking a mob of cattle from Quilpie in Queensland to Bourke, about seven to eight weeks' walk, when I heard that my brother Frank was taking 5,500 sheep down the Darling to Wentworth. He needed a lead dog, and as I could manage the cattle without Sandsoap, he went to the Vicn border on the sort of job he liked best.

Frank and I both arrived back at Bourke about the same time. There I got the bad news about Sandsoap. Having finished the job to Wentworth, and coming home back up the road along the Darling, Sandsoap fell off the back of the truck and was found hanging lifelessly by his collar.

Frank said he was in a hurry to catch the punt over the river at

Louth before the operator headed for the pub. One of his men had found the dog when he checked the load. He unhooked Sandsoap and put his body somewhere off to the side of the road.

I really missed that dog when I had nearly 8,000 sheep going down the Darling and across to Swan Hill on the Vicn border. It was some three months after Sandsoap was hanged. I crossed over the punt at Louth and was heading down the west side of the Darling.

I reached Dunlop Station with those 8,000 sheep and a team of sore-footed dogs, to find very little feed. A fellow from the Station came down the road on horseback, followed by a dog. As he came level with the front of my mob about half a mile from the tail, I saw a dog branch off and go across the lead. The bloke I had up on the other wing near the lead started coming back and the bloke that was to pilot us through came on down to the tail where I was. We both arrived on the tail of the mob about the same time. The station man told me he'd left his dog up at the lead as it was the only place he'd work. My man remarked that he was a good lead dog, too.

This station bloke and I rode along behind the sheep, him telling me about his dog in the lead, and me telling him about my dog Sandsoap, and how they worked very much the same. You never would see much of them, but you knew they were up there as the lead was being kept square across the face and every now and then would be bumped back. Everything Sandsoap could do, this bloke's dog, Bandy, could do, and I was beginning to think that this bloke was a parrot. I had thought there wasn't another dog in the country that could work as well as Sandsoap. Everyone that knew him reckoned he was the best dog they'd ever seen.

We were pulling into dinner camp and I said to this bloke, 'Pull your dog in, mate, and give him a blow and a drink.'

'He'll come in when the sheep start to camp,' he said.

By this time, I felt like hanging one on him because Sandsoap also wouldn't leave the sheep until the sheep had started to camp.

'Do you want to sell him?' I said. 'I could use a good lead dog and you could buy another good dog for five pounds.' So I offered him ten. The station bloke said he was not for sale.

Just then, the dog came from behind and I couldn't believe my eyes. The dog was the same colour, black and tan, and had the same goggle eyes. The bloke called him Bandy and it was heading for him. I was at the campfire twenty yards off the line the dog was taking when the bloke called again, 'Bandy'. I called, 'Sandsoap'.

The dog stopped and came straight for me, jumping all over me, wagging and grinning like mad.

The bloke from the station said, 'You must have a way with dogs. That's the first time I've seen him go near anyone else.'

I said, 'We've been talking about the same dog all morning.'

He said, 'It can't be. You said your brother had him when he was hanged.'

'That's right,' I said. 'But it was only 25 miles back along the road to Louth where he was supposed to have been dumped. He must've been just unconscious. How long have you had this dog?'

'I came five months ago and was here about a month when the dog turned up. He was very sick and couldn't eat much.'

He asked how long it had been since my brother was through here. I told him it had been three months and three weeks.

'Are you sure he's your dog?' he asked. 'Prove he's your dog.'

I said, 'You send him around the sheep and I'll stop him within ten feet without calling his name.'

He sent him. The dog had just started to gallop when I gave a sharp whistle. The dog went down to ground. I told him to send the dog around the sheep again. This time I let the dog get further away, and I stopped him again. 'This time you stop him by name.'

The dog ran off and the bloke called out 'Bandy'. Then again, 'Bandy'. I let the dog go until he was at the sheep, then whistled. Down went the dog.

The bloke got up and said, 'He's yours, all right.'

'Yes, a bloody ghost dog,' I said.

The station bloke left the camp minus Sandsoap, but with twenty pounds in his pocket. After that, Sandsoap was known around the drovers' camps as the ghost dog.

Hazell is a red and tan kelpie who lives on a property near Neilrex, 100 kilometres from Dubbo. Here she's at the West Wyalong Yard Dog Trials in August 2013 at the age of fourteen months, showing her great concentration. She was quick to keep the sheep on the move and to follow them out of the race and onto the next part of the round. **Lorraine Williams, West Wyalong, NSW**

Boots has eye and plenty of it: once he has locked on to a few breakaways, there is no escaping his skill. He is never far from his boss and loves the kids when they give him cuddles. **Arlie McCumstie, Goodooga, NSW**

A drover's mate

Des Coombes Coffs Harbour, NSW

Dan was a true drover's mate. I'm not sure how my father acquired him, and his parentage was never established apart from having a fair bit of kelpie in him. But there was no doubting his working ability.

My father often drove a mob of bullocks from the Kempsey area and through the town of Macksville for slaughter at the abattoirs, a distance of 50 kilometres. Dan was his only help. Without ever having to be told, Dan would block and direct the cattle in any problem areas along the way.

His reputation became so great that people would come out of their houses and shops in Macksville to watch Dan shepherd the stock through the town and over the bridge. If you know the town of Macksville you would realise how difficult the task was. Dan never missed a trouble spot or lost a bullock.

During the 1940s, when droving was the common way of moving mobs of cattle, a good cattle dog was a prized possession, especially when it was paramount to get stock to abattoirs in a non-stressed state. On at least two occasions Dan was stolen, but each time an observant citizen would report to my father that he had seen Dan chained up at some farm in the district and Dan would be retrieved, happy to be back home.

Queenie with the dashing tongue

Louella Vaughan Mogilla, NSW

A droving friend of mine, Ted, had a red kelpie called Queenie. On quiet command she would be sent to turn the head or bring up the rear of the roving mobs.

In the full heat of summer, far from dams and creeks where cattle often break and run, I've seen Queenie work to hold the mob until she was staggering from thirst and exhaustion. Ted's hardy old Akubra would then quickly be adapted to make a water bowl to revive her.

At home after the evening meal was finished, a chair would sometimes be pulled up—'but not too near the table'—for Queenie. The mock kissing game which ensued would keep us all amused as the bespectacled, leathery face of the drover would tease his sleek, seal-like kelpie.

Her head would bow in false and knowing modesty, her eyes turned upward coyly at her owner, watching for that opportunity for her dashing tongue to make contact with the cheek that came so temptingly close, then jerked away. Affection masked by chastisement would follow: 'By Jesus, Queenzy, don't you go kissin' me.'

Her head would drop and the kelpie grin would turn to a Mona Lisa smile as she played the game over and over again and just now and then had a win, only to be called a 'dirty old thing'.

After the games, she'd be rewarded with a bone off a plate and would depart with a majestic air that indicated she really did understand the meaning of her name.

Together, somewhere in Queensland they took a mob. The day was hot, the grass was good and sheep had spread for what seemed like miles. Queenie was sent to bring them to check. She was on her way a 'long way back'. The rate of the dust rising from the road told Ted that a car was coming at a furious pace. He reckoned the driver would slow down when he realised the front stragglers were part of a mob. But he did not.

Too far away to warn Queenie, but close enough to witness the impact, Ted's heart missed a beat as he saw that she was hit. In rage he picked up a rock and hurled it at the passing car, shattering the windscreen. Still the driver did not bother to stop and Ted's curses were drowned out by the engine's roar.

Mounting his horse, he urged it through the settling dust to where Queenie lay.

'Sweet Jesus, why?' he whispered.

He took his pocket knife from its pouch and crouching over Queenie, slit her down the side. She had been heavily in pup and he thought one might just be alive.

The souped-up car and angry young driver returned with policeman in tow. The drover's weathered face was stony and white and the dust on it was wet and smeared from sweat—or tears.

In his trembling hands he still held the knife and in the other a fine, fat, lifeless pup, one from a litter of eight, their helpless bodies spread on the ground.

Punch was a red and tan kelpie bred and trained by my mother, Perina Giles, who used him on the farm and for trialling. He'd do anything for her, including jumping over a fence again and again so that Tom could get a perfectly focused photo. Mum was one of the first women to get involved in trialling kelpie dogs along with her identical twin sister, Erin Caterson. Mum is 77 now but we have a great photo of her in the 1960s trialling at Goondiwindi, wearing a mini-skirt and knee-high suede lace-up boots. Punch died last year. Mum still has a few dogs left, although she hasn't trialled for a while. I can't imagine Mum without her kelpies. **Tom Keating;** photo sent in by **Perina Giles** (daughter), **Goulburn, NSW**

Mr Brooks and Blue

Jeff Baldwin Wangaratta, Vic

An old man as I remember him, Mr Brooks was the last of the bullockies in our area, the Dandenongs, between 1920 and 1930. Contrary to the popular image of bullockies, he was not loud-mouthed, nor did he swear. Instead he was a kindly, softly spoken man who got things done quietly and efficiently. To my knowledge he had always been a bullock driver.

I daresay he sensed my love for bullocks and dogs, and that's why I was allowed to tag along.

Mr Brooks had a kelpie-cross Queensland heeler called Blue. I was allowed to follow along behind the wagon (bare feet in the dust or mud) and turn the wheel that operated the brake.

When Mr Brooks was yoking his bullocks for the day's work, Blue would heel the bullocks with such ferocity that they would just stand and watch him, too frightened to move away and avoid the yokes being put on.

These days it's hard to visualise an old man yoking up a team of between twelve and twenty bullocks single-handedly and without yards, but that's what Mr Brooks did with Blue. The dog would stand by and watch, until asked to take action on any beast that would not get into line.

After the team was yoked and hitched to whatever load they were asked to pull, Blue really came into his own. Bullocks are like humans—they will bludge if given the chance. When this happened, it only needed Mr Brooks to say 'Baldy', 'Ring', 'Brindle', whatever the name was of the offending beast, and Blue would slip in behind the 'bludger', usually unseen, and provide the necessary incentive to correct the bullock's laziness.

In most cases it was not necessary for the dog to heel the guilty bullock because as soon as Mr Brooks spoke its name, it knew what the result would be should it not respond.

I have been working dogs all my life and still am. When I set the gates a certain way, a bitch will muster a 150-acre paddock; when I rub the knife on the steel, a dog will bring in the killers; when bringing up the house cows, the dogs will leave the dry cows behind—and so it goes on. Most farmers have dogs that respond to a given situation.

However, on reflection over the years, Mr Brooks and Blue seem to me to have been the most perfect combination. The dog Blue made it possible for that old man to carry on his profession right up to almost the end of his life. He never had to rely on other people, and more importantly, he did not draw on the public purse for social service, pension or whatever—thanks to Blue, who only ever asked to be fed.

First encounter: Tex at the age of five months, at our farm near Wondai. While we were busy yard building, he was wandering around checking out everything, as curious pups do, and a mob of bullocks came to see what we were up to. Tex casually approached the bullocks and just sat staring at the cattle. To my amazement, the cattle and pup just froze and I was able to capture this moment. **Lauren Cross, Kingaroy, Qld**

Droving up to Onslow

Peter Richardson Toodyay, WA

I was in the pastoral game in the Gascoyne for a good number of years and owned and saw many dogs. This story is about a red cloud dog of mine called Rusty. In the late 1940s, when I was twenty-three, four of us were contracted by Elders to take a mob of sheep from Carnarvon to Onslow. It was a distance of more than 400 miles on back tracks to collect wethers from properties along the way, to be shipped to the Middle East. We collected the first mob from a property called Wandagee. From there we went up the track to Midialia, Williambury and Lyndon to end up with about 2,000 head. We followed the Lyndon River most of the way, and as it was winter we had plenty of water for the trip, which took in total about five weeks. For most of the way, the going was terribly rough.

Each man had a dog and of the four, Rusty was the best. As well as our stock horses, we had two pack horses and a cart pulled by two other horses and a mule. On the cart we carried all the swags, cooking gear and food, as well as big rolls of hessian with which we made temporary night yards for the sheep using steel droppers to keep it in place.

About twenty miles out of Lyndon, the track was so rocky and rough that our cart broke an axle and fell apart. We had no choice but to load all the gear from the cart onto the two cart horses and the mule. Since we had no spare pack saddles, we had to use the most extraordinary improvisations imaginable. We folded the hessian over each animal and bundled droppers each side and tied the rest of the gear on top. In this fashion, we continued on with the sheep to Onslow.

Once we'd delivered the sheep and rested up, we set out on our long trip back to Carnarvon to return the plant. Normally the dogs would have travelled home on the cart after their weeks of work, but because we had no cart, they had to walk. About halfway between Onslow and Lyndon, the dogs were so tired and footsore, they could not travel any further. We couldn't carry them on the horses because of all the extra gear we had to carry, so we had no choice but to leave them there on the track—much to my sorrow. Some weeks later we reached Carnarvon and I returned to Wooramel, where I was the overseer.

About two or three weeks later, I got a phone call from Tim D'Arcy, the manager at Lyndon, to say my dog Rusty had turned up there. I felt this was remarkable as he had obviously pushed on after me as best he could. He must have come the best part of 100 miles.

Tim D'Arcy put him on the mail truck and I picked him up in Carnarvon. We enjoyed many a good year together after I thought I had lost him. None of the other dogs made it back.

The collie team ready for a day's work in the Glastonbury Creek Valley. **Wade Kerle, Shelly Beach, Qld**

133

Reliable Dart

Linda Irwin Casino, NSW

Dart was a red kelpie owned by Herb Dunn and he was descended from the first dog he brought to the far north coast of New South Wales in about 1910. There are thousands of kelpies up there now and most owners would claim they are descendants of Dart.

While Herb and Whispering Jack, an Aboriginal stockman, were asleep under a tarpaulin, their mob of 200 bullocks 'rushed'. Hearing the roaring noise, they mounted their horses bareback and galloped after them, hoping to eventually catch up and turn them. They were surprised to go only two kilometres before finding the panting bullocks and the dog standing quietly. Dart had gone, without direction, and turned them into a two-rail fence.

Herb often took mobs of cattle, mostly young or bullocks up to 1,000 head, through Casino with its many streets, lanes and empty blocks. He would steady the lead, and Dart, needing no instructions, would keep the mob moving by racing up one side, peering through the moving legs, and when the cattle broke away on the other side he would race around the tail and bring them together.

Herb often had to take cattle over the Richmond River at Coraki. He would notify the punt operator who in turn would warn travellers that the punt would be disrupted on a certain day.

One particular day Herb, with Hilary Lulham, a lad of sixteen, mustered 400 young steers and drove them to the landing area to get there just on daylight. Dart and 25 head were first on, and with a few whistles, Herb directed them to an area away from the punt landing. Each trip took half an hour. Dart met each load and kept the mob together without any further directions. The whole operation took ten hours and it was dark when the cattle were driven to a holding paddock.

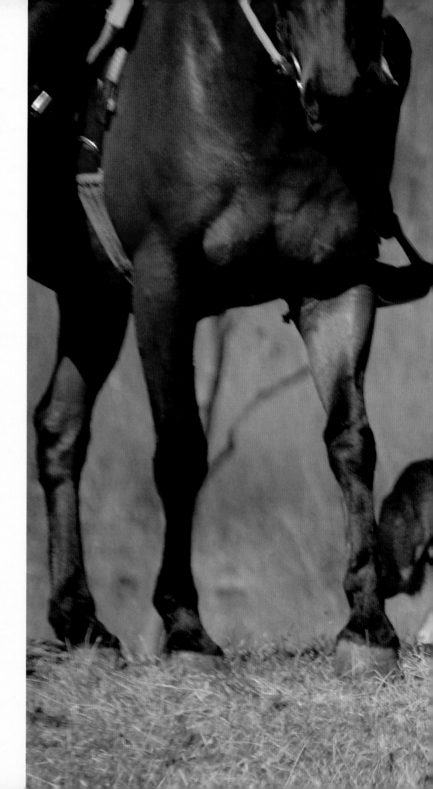

Out on the job. It's hot, it's dry, and tongues are hanging out for the next water trough, but Tub, Brandy and Bette are still ready and anxious to finish the job. They enjoy a short break now that the mob has been gathered, and they settle in beside the horse, waiting for further instructions. **Bronwyn Burnham, Eidsvold, Qld**

Gordon, a black and tan kelpie, was one of the funniest dogs we've had the pleasure of owning. Workwise, you'd describe him as a handy paddock and yard dog rather than a top all-rounder. He was a big dog and didn't like the shed. The skill he did have was catching flyblown sheep in the mob. He got so good at it, he was able to catch struck sheep in the paddock, sometimes without command. This saved us from having to bring the full mob to the yards to treat isolated sheep. The command we'd give him was: 'Grab 'im, Gordon, grab 'im.' He liked to run behind the quad bike through the farm. One day, running down a drainage channel bank with little water in it, large carp were clearly visible, so the command was given: 'Grab 'im, Gordon, grab 'im.' Amazingly, he did. Caught a big carp, the width of the bike rack, and dragged it up the bank. This became an enjoyable pastime for him, watching out for carp and jumping out of a moving vehicle to fish. If we were taking sheep through the farm and there were carp to be found, where was Gordon when you needed him? Gone fishin'. **Brian and Libby Bailey, Murrami, NSW**

So she wouldn't be left behind

G H Harkin Halifax, Qld

My father was a drover from 1910 till late 1960. He had numerous stories of working dogs, the kelpie breed mostly, as they were the dogs that knew the job well, were very hardy, reliable, intelligent and obedient to the drover's command.

He had been camped for a while between jobs. The red kelpie bitch meantime had produced puppies and kept them near a tree, some way from the camp. When Dad had to move off to pick up his next flock of sheep, he started to pack up and harness his horses.

Suddenly he noticed a small puppy on the track to the bitch's tree. He picked it up and returned it to the tree, but found that others were missing.

The dog apparently had noticed the movements in the camp signalling they would soon be off. She had taken it upon herself to load her puppies into a wire basket under the wagon—the usual place for pups when the droving outfit was on the move.

Our border collie Millie's first litter of pups: three black and whites, one chocolate and white, and one blue and white. At six weeks we put them in the back of the truck to go to the vet to have their first immunisations. They were so excited to be out in the big wide world; little did they know what was to come. **Anita Juffermans, Warburton, Vic**

The dogs of old Glen Helen

Bryan Bowman Alice Springs, NT

When, in 1938, I took over Glen Helen from Fred Raggatt, he had an old dog called Whiskey and an old bitch called Rosie. Rosie was mothering her last litter of puppies.

Raggatt left the old dog and Rosie with me, plus three pups, as he was leaving the Territory for good and going to live in Adelaide.

In three months, the pups—Bully, Snowy and Daisy—were following me through all classes of stock work, though admittedly I sometimes had to carry one of them home in front of me on the horse after a very long day.

Nineteen thirty-eight was a dry year on the north side of the MacDonnell Ranges but in January 1939, a big monsoonal rain caused high flooding in the Fink River. This didn't worry the dogs. We crossed a big mob of station horses over the Fink in a relatively shallow spot with the water just up to their wither. The dogs swam the river attaching themselves to any horses hanging back, keeping them bunched up and moving along.

Ten inches fell in one week, followed by a further six inches in February. By April there were plenty of cattle ready for market and we started mustering. We got most of the cattle without having to get out of a walk very often.

Nineteen thirty-nine was such a good season that with the assistance of the dogs, the whole herd, including the big cleanskins, was branded and the fat cattle sent to market. War had broken out in Europe and a military camp had grown up in Alice Springs bringing restrictions on sending cattle out of the Northern Territory. Unfortunately, the good rains of 1939 were not repeated in 1940. It proved to be one of the driest years on record. By November 1940, cattle were dying along the Fink and the whole area had to be destocked within walking distance of

the river. Most of this area had been completely eaten out. It had been overstocked for years in Raggatt's time, but there had been no alternative at that time as he had no other permanent water supply.

When we opened up two wells on the station, it was still a 45-mile walk to the nearest one. That's a long way in the heat without water for weak cattle.

However, we got there by waiting for the full moon and travelling through the night. There were minimal losses. We put the cattle together on the Fink about two days before the full moon, gave them a good drink at about five o'clock in the afternoon, had supper and moved off into the copper and gold sunset with the moon now well above the horizon and the dogs bringing up the rear. If at any time a cow or a calf lay down in the scrub, you would hear a commotion and a calf would rush past you back into the mob while the dogs, looking very pleased with themselves, would be eagerly looking for the next one to hang back.

We moved some 2,000 cattle from the Fink area and saved that country around the Fink from being damaged during that terrible year.

I have tried since then to establish a good breed of cattle dog without success.

The day of the cattle dog in the Centre for mustering is over, but they are still used a bit for yard work. Dogs of today ride in vehicles and their feet get too soft. A day's work in the Ranges is about all they can stand. Also, most of the mustering is done today with helicopters and dogs mainly flush out cattle hiding in thick clumps of scrub.

Boss on the left and George on the right, at Hillside Station, 90 kilometres south of Marble Bar, WA. In 2008 my wife and I called in to say hello, but we ended up doing a full mustering season there. George was the oldest of the working dogs, but he soon showed the younger ones how it was done. **Laurie Owens, Tomerong, NSW**

Scenting the way

Tom Robinson Wilmington, SA

My story comes from an era when working dogs really earned their tucker. It was during the war years when petrol was rationed and prior to 'Ag' bikes. At that time, we had two female working dogs, sisters named Brownie and Kitty, and they never worked on the same side of a mob of sheep.

Dad and I were mustering various paddocks to get together fat lambs for railing to Gepps Cross market. The railway siding was at the small town of Hammond. Our property more or less surrounded the town.

Our first job this day was to take a mob of sheep from a paddock six miles west of Hammond. As we got them out on the road, one of the sheep wouldn't walk, so we loaded it into the back of the utility.

We left Brownie to take this mob of sheep to the railway yards. We then drove the sheep that wouldn't walk to these yards, and proceeded to another paddock that was located six miles east of the town to muster the sheep held there. Having completed this task, we then walked them towards the railway yards and were about one mile from Hammond when we met Brownie with her mob.

The local Postmaster at Hammond later told us that he saw Brownie bring her mob into the town, every now and then going ahead and smelling the ground to find the scent of our ute. In the middle of the town she turned the mob at the crossroads and detoured up to the railway yards (where we had unloaded the lame sheep) and not finding us there, again turned the mob and followed our tracks back through the town with the sheep, turned at the crossroads and proceeded on to meet us.

Nowadays, the increase in road traffic and public liability insurance risk would not allow such a feat as this to occur.

Ginny (tri-coloured collie) and Boots (kelpie cross) helping to muster goats into the yards, ready for drafting and trucking. Ginny is our lead dog, and Boots is always there to back her up and lend a bit of muscle to convince the goats to go where we need them. **Cathy Zwick, Cooladdi, Qld**

Beyond price

David de Bomford Forth, Tas

In the late 1920s my family lived on a farm on the old Surrey Road at Romaine, south of Burnie. My father owned a female border collie sheepdog which he had trained to drove sheep unaccompanied. On one occasion when he had bought sheep at the Cooee saleyard, my father sent them on their way and left the dog to take them home—a distance of about five miles.

My father had business to attend to and returned home via a different route. When the dog did not arrive with the sheep at the expected time, he went in search of them. He found them about halfway home and wondered why the dog had taken such a long time. An explanation was provided later by a local farmer who had seen the dog alone with the sheep and had watched her at work.

There had been a lame sheep in the flock and rather than hustle it along, the dog would allow it to have a spell at frequent intervals. She would let the rest of the sheep wander on but she was careful not to let them get too far ahead. She would bring them back to the lame one, gather it into the flock and urge it on a little bit further. Again and again she shepherded the sheep to and fro, all the while taking care to ensure that the lame sheep was given sufficient rest to allow it to continue.

Although the continual rounding up of the sheep and the backtracking with them must have wearied the dog, her patience never flagged. Her efforts not only kept the flock intact but ensured that the lame sheep did not just make the journey, but did so with the minimum of discomfort.

The farmer was so impressed with the dog's capability that he offered to buy the dog for a substantial sum of money. My father would not sell her. She was beyond price.

After the hustle and bustle of a morning's trade, stockmen get together for a quick catch-up … and their dogs do the same.
Sally Harding, Albury, NSW

Left in the dark

Les Brooks Barraba, NSW

After spending 60 years in Sydney, I came to Barraba to become a wool grower and cattle breeder. One day I had to do repairs along the boundary fence, so set off with my motorbike and border collie, Sonnee. I found a large hole in the fence in the south-east corner of the property and set to work on the necessary repairs.

The repairs took me ages. It was only when I had finished that I realised how late in the day it was. It was so dark that I had to feel for my tools on the ground. I couldn't even see my hand out in front of me. I turned around and started to walk back to my motorbike but found, to my horror, that it was so dark I had no idea where it was.

Realising the seriousness of the situation—I had never been to that part of the property before—I felt that my only hope of getting out of there was to call Sonnee. It was one of those dense black nights—no moon, cloudy sky—and bitterly cold for we were at 2,000 feet in the New England area in the month of August.

I called but nothing happened. I called a little louder. Nothing. Then, feeling the panic rising, I called at the top of my voice. I was relieved to hear a rustle in the bushes and feel him brush my legs. I knelt down, put my arm around his neck and said, 'Sonnee, I'm lost.' I then asked him to take me back to the motorbike.

He immediately set off and I followed the sound of him rustling the bushes. Sure enough, he led me straight back to the bike.

I knew we were there by the smell of petrol which had been leaking from the carburettor.

I patted him, thanked him for leading me back to the bike and said, 'Now, my boy, you'll have to take me back to the homestead.' For that was my next problem. When I started the bike the headlights immediately came on, but although the track through the heavily timbered ironbark could be found easily in daylight, it was impossible to recognise at night. Everything looked the same. So once again I was totally lost.

Sonnee had already taken off, so again I had to call out to him but, as before, I had to call out three times and at the top of my voice. Then came the familiar rustle of the bushes and the brushing against my legs. Once again I got down on my knees, but this time I put both arms around his neck.

'Sonnee, I'm really lost,' I said. 'Take me back to the homestead.'

So off he went, but this time he only went a few yards before he stopped, turned around and looked back to see if I was still following. He did this all the way back—even at the public roadway where normally, during the day, he would try to beat me back home over the last 1.5 kilometres. This time he kept stopping, looking back and ensuring I was still following.

I got home, cold but safe and eternally thankful. I quite forgive him for not being the world's greatest worker.

At the Yard Dog Trials, Gunning Show. **Dave Harris, Downer, ACT**

Happy Father's Day

Geoffrey Blight Narrogin, WA

It was a few years ago now, and just two days before Father's Day. The phone rang, summoning me to Busselton Hospital, 200 kilometres away. My father had just been admitted, unconscious after collapsing at his home.

A third-generation sheep man, Dad had retired three years earlier after being struck down with a heart attack on the family farm. After a short hospital stay Dad had hung up his boots and took Mum, who was also in poor health, and they went paddling together in the sea, to live out their remaining life.

For Dad, that break away was not like him at all as the farm had been his beginning and, simply, his life—a life totally dedicated to his family of three, and twelve grandchildren.

It had also been a life of love and dependence on the land, the sheep, the dogs and the horses that he had shared his 67 years with. All these he left behind after that first hospital stay.

What we didn't know, because he told no-one, was that he had cancer and he felt he owed it to Mum, something she had desired, and earned over 44 years—a rest and some friends to talk and share a break with from the never-ending battle against the problems people on the land face.

And so they went, not looking back as they said goodbye, everyone not really understanding but still happy for them, all bar Rusty—and Rusty missed Dad.

Rusty was an ageing farm dog, a big, red, long-haired mongrel kelpie who had worked with Dad every single day for about nine years. Dad was a hard master—the dog went on the chain at night, he was not allowed inside and he did as he was told. But Dad loved him and he shared those working days with him, morning to night. Every hour of light they were together.

Fencing, driving sheep, whatever it was, there they were, the old ute, Dad and his dog.

There was nothing for a dog like Rusty where Dad was going, only the chain, and that wasn't the way a man likes to see his best friend end, so they had to say goodbye.

Rusty worked those three years after Dad left, a bit here, a bit there, but it wasn't the same. Often I would find him sitting on the disused old ute, just looking, just waiting, just hoping.

At the hospital they told me that they had already done investigative surgery. Dad had massive abdominal cancer, his bowels were blocked. He had been fitted with artificial pipes and bags, but his chances of more than a few days were very remote. Mum wanted me to tell him rather than the doctor. She felt I might be more of a comfort to him.

Because of the drugs and the operation Dad was too dazed to talk to that day. I had shared the ride with my sister to the hospital so I was obliged to borrow my father's car to return to the farm, and then drive back again on Father's Day, to see him through to the end.

The car sat in the yard next day and an old dog strutted around and around it, ever watchful, looking and waiting, fighting any canine that was game to draw too near. The scent was strong, his hopes were up but the hand or the voice never came.

I lay awake all night and pondered how and what to say to my father. 'Thank you, Dad. I love you. Goodbye. God bless and Happy Father's Day,' but nothing came and with dawn I just felt confusion and sadness as we prepared to leave.

A phone call from Mum told me that Dad was being allowed home for an hour to share Father's Day with his entire family, who

My work dogs have plenty of fun on play days: trips to the beach, competing at three-sheep trialling and the odd day at the Royal Show showing how clever they are. They are my mates and one of the reasons I find sheep farming such an enjoyable living.
Karyn Buller, Darkan, WA

by now had begun gathering, and still the words wouldn't come. 'Remember the old days, Dad. Don't worry, Dad. We won't forget you, Dad.' They just weren't right.

Dressed and ready to go as dawn broke I stood by the car door, looking down on the ageing dog while waiting for all the family to get themselves settled in the car. The sad, disappointed eyes still searching, looking, hoping, pleading.

I opened the door and for what reason I still don't know, I told the old dog to get in. The ears came up, the scent was stronger, it had been a long time since he had sat in there. Maybe, just maybe.

All hell broke loose when my well-dressed family now had to share space with the hairy old dog.

'Why in the name of fortune does he have to go? There's no room. Don't be stupid. Get that dog out of the car.'

The spur of the moment idea didn't enjoy any support and matters didn't improve when we reached Busselton.

'What are you going to do with the dog? There's nowhere to put him. He'll start a fight with Rex. Get him out of here.' And so, after three hours of hoping, Rusty was bundled into the garden shed, out of the way, before we went to get Dad for that precious hour.

He looked very sick, very tired. He coughed blood every few minutes as he tried to smile and to be happy but he knew, he had known all along, that this day would come. At least he had made Mum happy these last three years and they had been happy— the walks, the swims, the grandchildren, the peace, and time to remember.

We put Dad on a bed in the lounge room, propped up with pillows. Grandchildren everywhere, muted chatter—'How are

147

you? . . . Anything I can get you? . . . Hello, Poppa.'

Everyone wanted to speak but no-one could think of what to say. All were uneasy. I went for a walk on the beach. I could take it no longer.

Later they told me they were going to have some photos taken of the grandchildren with Pop when the barking started. Pop, needing something to say, asked to see Rex, Mum's pet Labrador, which was making most of the noise. Mum let Rex inside. He sent things flying as he bounded around everyone, forcing them out of his way and so had to be banned outside to the shed, with a departing smile and a pat from Dad.

No-one had mentioned Rusty and Mum didn't know what to do as Rusty had never been in a house in his life. Dad never spoke of him but here, eyes shining at her, his old ears up, Rusty was pleading to be let out.

Twenty people stood in the lounge room, the camera ready. They were about to take a picture we could all remember, one last shot of Pop and the family he loved. Everyone was restrained. They kept looking away, the words just wouldn't come.

Then another entered the room. He came quietly and fast, his head held high, the eyes glistening, ears up, now the scent was stronger. Between the legs he came. All stared but no-one said a word. The old dog only looked ahead, tail wagging, and then their eyes met.

Only the old dog moved, a slight bound and four hairy paws rested on the bed. Glistening eyes stared at each other in a silent room. As the long nose reached out, the soft moist tongue touched a hardened old cheek, the tears, shining and silent, joined together and rolled uncontrolled down a very sick but happy face.

It was then I met all the family walking quietly along the beach. They had left what was left of the hour to Mum, Dad and Rusty.

When we did return to the house it was time for me to take Dad back to hospital. Nobody touched or spoke to Rusty. He just sat by the bed and as we moved Dad into a wheelchair, out he followed.

Everyone was saying goodbye or volunteering to go back with him to the hospital, but Dad just smiled and thanked them and beckoned Rusty into the back of the car, asking that only he accompany us.

I could not say anything as we drove the four miles back. I stole a glance occasionally at the strained faces looking forward, the old dog now standing on the back seat, his nose only inches from the old man's cheek.

Nothing whatsoever was said between man and dog. At the hospital entrance I lifted Dad into the wheelchair. He stared straight ahead. No words, not even a glance at Rusty. As I moved the chair back to shut the car door, the old dog sat, nose pressed hard against the glass. Still the old man stared ahead, now visibly upset and trembling.

For a moment I thought I might say something but could not. As I started to push the chair away an old hand suddenly came out and bony old fingers pressed hard against the glass. Their eyes met for the last time and in a moment not meant for me, the old man, tears streaming freely down his cheeks, mumbled, 'Goodbye, old boy,' and we slowly moved away.

They are both dead now. Dad was carried to his final resting place by his tearful young grandsons, his witness read solemnly and sincerely by loving grand-daughters.

On the last page of a family album that spans 44 years of a happy and very successful marriage is a picture of an old man, tears staining his cheeks, his hands outstretched to his workmate, his friend, taken in the lounge room on that final Father's Day. A loving family left all the words to a hairy old dog to deliver.

Heading home on Brooking Springs Station near Fitzroy Crossing in the remote Kimberley region of WA. It was 120 kilometres from the back of the station to the homestead, along a dusty farm track. I hung out the window of the speeding ute and snapped this picture at a slow speed to create the motion blur effect while maintaining the right dog's gaze. You can sense a connection between the dog and the photographer, which is aided by having the eyes very in focus and the other dogs slightly out of focus. I think it shows the true spirit and loyalty of the working dog. **Rocky Sutherland, Kununurra, WA**

A last farewell

Nyree Renney Berriwillock, Vic

As we headed off to Nandaly, we knew we had a sad day ahead of us. Pat Conlan, the father of a very close friend of ours, had died suddenly on the Sunday night from a heart attack at the age of fifty-three.

Arriving at the funeral, we weren't surprised to see five to six hundred people. Pat had been a pillar of the local community, a leading farmer in the district, and a wonderful husband and father to six strapping sons.

However, we were surprised to see a sheepdog tied to the church gate. He was greeted by a few as they went through to the small country church and we decided he must have been Pat's working dog.

A few hundred people were standing outside the church and as the service conducted by Father Coffey went along, we all became more and more aware of the dog. Each time the congregation was asked to pray, the dog would howl. After a reading or eulogy was finished, he would howl again.

To this day, I feel a wonderment at the dog's action—although, after all, he had probably spent as much time with Pat as anyone. One certainly got the feeling that Patrick Conlan and his dog had been soul mates.

The dog continued on with the family to the cemetery and once again acted as though he were grieving for his master.

At the luncheon after the funeral, the dog arrived again and was put in the kindergarten playground. He was a little lighter-hearted there.

Everyone who attended the funeral commented at some time on this dog and his actions. They also commented on what a moving and loving tribute to her husband it was for Marie to remember the dog at such a tragic time and give him an opportunity to say a last farewell to his master and very obviously best mate. It was the most moving funeral I've ever been to. The dog's name was Oscar.

Night muster

Zita Ward Singleton, NSW

This is a tribute to a black kelpie sheepdog named Digger. During the late 1930s we lived on a farm which was situated at the end of the road, and well off the beaten track. It included a valley with a creek which forked into three separate narrow valleys. Each valley was separated by high, and quite rugged, wooded hills, mostly unfenced.

It was a very pretty place, quiet and full of tranquillity—except for the dingoes which seemed to have arrived en masse very soon after we stocked up with sheep. Their attacks on our flock became so bad we were forced to yard all the sheep each night.

This proved a difficult task for us with only my father to do it, plus help from my eleven-year-old brother and me, aged sixteen. We had several dogs who would work well for anyone, but Digger was a new, young dog being trained by Dad, and not allowed to go with us kids.

One night my father was called away from home overnight, which left the mustering to us. Our mother arranged to do the valley near our house, and since she did not ride a horse, she had to walk a few kilometres into the rough foothills. She decided to take Digger with her, hoping he would understand her inadequate instructions, in place of Dad, who had a mighty voice and a whistle which carried a power of authority.

Just on dusk my brother and I arrived back at the house after yarding our mob, only to find our mother was not yet back. We rode up the valley to meet her and found that she had lost Digger in the scrub. Obviously he had moved out of earshot as our calling and whistling failed to get a response.

By now it was quite dark. The area was so rugged and dangerous for anyone not very familiar with it that we were forced to give up and hope that Digger could find his way back home. We had already lost a few dogs who had been enticed to follow the dingo pack and had never returned. Our father would be most upset if we had lost Digger.

About 9 pm we heard strange noises at the back gate of our house yard. There we found Digger holding a small flock of about 50 sheep in a tight circle.

The dog, being still young, was quite knocked up and glad of a late feed. We were overjoyed to have him back, and also to have the sheep safely home since more than likely they would have been victims of the wild dogs, who persistently waited for a chance to maul any strays.

It was an incredible feat for a lone dog to have shepherded sheep out of that steep, rough country and several kilometres back to the house.

After a long day Michael and his hard-working kelpie, Buddy, had just finished feeding grain to some very hungry sheep. Michael and Buddy had mobs of sheep to move closer to water, as the dams in the back paddocks were getting pretty low. **Robin Flattery, Hay, NSW**

Looking for The Word. The cattle are being yarded, and Turbo looks to Lance for confirmation that the job has been completed. **Bronwyn Burnham, Eidsvold, Qld**

Ginger

Helen Best Barraba, NSW

We had a regular shearer, John, who was a friend of the family. He always brought his dog Ginger with him while he was at our shed for the weeks of shearing.

After several years, Ginger was a welcome temporary addition to our workforce and Dad began to rely on him being there.

One year, a few days after shearing finished, we were surprised to see Ginger on the doorstep again and ready for work. He had found his way back to our place, Fairview, seven miles from the town, on his own.

On the Friday night there was no sign of our extra dog. He had gone home to be with his owner.

Thus the pattern was set. Whenever John went to a big shed and left the dog in town, Ginger came out to Fairview and worked happily with us. He always only stayed until his owner returned to town, be it Friday night, or because of a break in routine because of rain and wet sheep. Ginger always knew. We never did work out how Ginger could possibly have known when John got back to town.

As 'our' dog grew older, the seven miles seemed to be too much for him, so he made the decision to make his home permanently at Fairview.

Little girl of the Bush

Jannial Thunguttie Kamilaroi Ashford, NSW

Since my old cat had mothered a variety of baby animals, I presented her with the two pups my friend and I had been promised. Their mother had been killed when they were one week old.

Beershee (meaning 'wild cat'—all my animals and birds get Aboriginal names), a grey, white and black tabby, sniffed around the tiny puppies, licked them and then pushed them towards her teats. My pup, Bami (meaning 'little girl'), was an Australian silky/Sydney silky/wirehaired terrier. When she was six months old we moved out onto a farm called Yurialawa, which was about 21 kilometres out of town. I went there to work as a jilleroo/caretaker/gardener.

From time to time, I would find Bami missing. The manager's wife told me she was with her husband. 'He loves your little dog,' she said. 'Have a look when he comes back.'

There she was in his saddlebag on the horse. Other times she would be up front on the saddle or sitting on the rump.

Bami used to team up with the working dogs when they rounded up sheep and cattle.

At one time, I was rounding up the sheep on foot and a Suffolk ram knocked me to the ground and would not let me up. I called the working dogs to help me but they didn't come. But Bami did, and she ran between his legs and grabbed hold of his testicles with her teeth and hung on for dear life. He turned around and around trying to shake her off him. No way could he get rid of her. Shaking with laughter, I shut the gate of the yards on the ram and called Bami. She let go and came to me. That ram never gave me trouble again.

About three months later the boss sold some old ewes and the stock truck came to pick them up. We had drafted off what we had wanted but then this same Suffolk ram somehow got into the yards and no way could we get him out. Not even the stock truck driver and his dogs could budge him. We tried the other dogs too, with no success.

'I know how to fix that ram,' I said, and called Bami. Well, you should have seen the look on his face—and did he move!

Jim, my boss, was amazed. 'That little dog is the only one that can manage that ram.'

The truck driver said he had seen all sorts of dogs work but nothing like Bami. He wanted to buy her, but not for anything was she for sale. Bami could work goats, cattle, sheep, horses, pigs and poultry.

How did she get there?

Doug Harkin Maryborough, Vic

I tell this story in an effort to solve a longstanding mystery. Between 25 and 35 years ago, I saw a border collie bitch lying beside the road at the intersection of the Talbot–Wareek and Maryborough–Avoca roads. The latter is now known as the Pyrenees Highway. This intersection is eight miles west of Maryborough and nine miles east of Avoca.

After about two days, the dog moved some 300 yards down to our house. It was very noticeable that one hind leg had about six inches cut off it. This looked to have been done by a mower or a binder. The dog's leg appeared to have been professionally repaired so I thought she must be a good dog, so I made every effort to locate the owner.

After feeding and watering her for a couple of days, during which she was very shy, I showed her a mob of sheep in the yards, but she did not seem interested.

I took them back to the paddock and called her. She very reluctantly followed me. When they were in the middle of the paddock I said, 'Go way back', and waved my arm. She flew around them with that particular hop and skip owing to one short leg. She stood up behind them and as I waved my arms she followed every order. From that moment she was my adoring slave and never left my side. If I was in the house, she would lie on the verandah and wait and listen. If I went out the back door she would be there in a flash. Wherever I worked she would curl up nearby but never let me move without her. When she knew which paddocks the sheep were in, and where the gates were, she could practically do all the sheep work herself. While travelling in a vehicle she was alert to danger and would warn the driver with a short whimper. At the house she announced a visitor with a single bark.

If I went away for a few days she would lie under an old sofa on the verandah and only eat enough to keep herself alive. When I came back she was back to her usual self.

My uncle once said, when trying to capture her attention, 'She won't take her eyes off you. She thinks you're bloody marvellous'.

We were inseparable for years and when she died I was very emotionally upset. She was the best and most faithful dog I have ever had in 70 years.

I have often wondered how she was left there—obviously not deliberately. Perhaps a truckie got out to inspect his load, and did not miss her on getting back. Surely, somewhere, there is someone still alive who knew of a marvellous border collie with three legs lost in that area. If so I would love to hear from them.

Dad with his mates Jake and Darcy, off to check the sheep after a day on the header.
Georgia Mattschoss, Barabba, SA

158

The story of Kate

Alex Haley Berrigan, NSW

I was travelling from my sheep farm at Tocumwal to Melbourne on a business trip when I stopped off at Wahring Cottage Service Station for fuel. John, the owner, came out to serve at the bowser, followed by his faithful corgi dog. But this morning there was an addition, a black and tan kelpie female about ten months old. She sat down just a couple of feet from my door to wait for the petrol to be served.

I looked at her and she looked at me and I guess she knew she had found her destiny. 'Who owns the kelpie, John?' I asked.

He said a bloke had dropped her off three weeks ago and was supposed to come back and pick her up. He hadn't shown up.

'I'll buy her off you,' I said. 'What's the price?'

'I'll ask the wife,' he said. 'And if she agrees, you can have her providing you bring her back if the owner turns up. Call back on your way home from Melbourne and if you promise a good home, I think you can have her.'

Seldom has the day taken so long to pass in Melbourne. I am usually short of time rushing from one venue to another and cursing because the day is going too quickly. My mind was with the little black and tan at Wahring. I conjured up in my imagination how, in my absence, the owner had returned to take her back—or worse, a truck had come in too fast and run over her.

I left Melbourne at 6 pm in the dark, and drove non-stop at the maximum speed the law would allow to cover the 130 kilometres as quickly as possible back to Wahring and the dog. Twenty kilometres before my destination, I eased back because I knew she had been killed or taken by someone else. I even felt anger that John hadn't given me the dog for safekeeping when I went to Melbourne that morning. I drove into the service station and couldn't believe my eyes. There, sitting out waiting for me it seemed, was the dog.

'Yes, she's yours, but a good home now.' John was all smiles as he knew that I wanted her. I opened the door of the car and, believe me or not, that dog knew she was going with me and jumped straight into the car.

'I'll be blowed,' John said. 'She hasn't accepted an offer to get into a car before, and she has been sitting at the end of the driveway entrance all day, as if she was waiting for you.'

'She's no good with sheep, you know,' John went on. 'The other bloke had a stock crate and she wouldn't work for him. Although he did say she was only ten months old.'

John's words had about the same effect as a bucket of cold water thrown over you unexpectedly on a hot day. 'She'll be right,' I muttered, a little flattened, and I drove away without a thank you to John.

She sat next to me. I told her her name was Kate and she rode like a lady in the car. When we reached home she walked inside.

At the sheep farm the next day, I did my immediate tasks quickly as I wanted to start Kate's training. About 60 weaners were ravaging the lucerne paddock, so there was a genuine job for Kate. Woody, my faithful friend, had no idea what to do with sheep but liked to come along and try. Woody accepted Kate into the household without fuss. The three of us went to the lucerne paddock and I pointed at the sheep and told Kate to 'go away back'.

Kate looked concerned but stood there. I said 'Go away back' again, and then, with Kate and Woody watching, I ran around the sheep. The neighbour yelled over the fence, 'The other way around, mate. You stand there and the dogs run around the sheep.'

Very bloody funny . . . the world's full of comedians. But foremost in my mind were John's parting words—'She's no good with sheep'. No good with sheep—hell, it doesn't matter. I like the dog anyway and I've managed without a dog this long—so what?

The sheep going out of the lucerne paddock turned left instead of right and ran the wrong way down the lane. 'Way back,' I shouted, and ran after the sheep to head them off. The sheep were fast and I was slowing and puffing and thinking I'd have to get the ute. A black and tan flash went past me to the front of the sheep and turned them, and then she stood there

No matter how isolated a farm is geographically, it is never a lonely place when it has a working dog or two. Christabel Gurr with her pals Kimba and Choco at Brukunga, South Australia. **Sally Harding, Albury, NSW**

looking back, sending the message, 'What the hell do I do now?'

'Bring 'em up,' I coaxed. She stood there. 'Push 'em up,' I pleaded. She stood there. 'Bark!' I yelled. 'Ruff, ruff.'

Woody rushed to the sheep as she knew about barking, and barked. Kate barked too, and the sheep ran. Kate began running from side to side, and I realised that I now had myself a sheepdog.

Times are tough. The economy of the farm is on a sharp downhill slide with no bottom in sight. Every day things go up, fuel costs rise, wool prices drop, and every other person who can only survive by increasing his charges is doing so. The only way I was going to save this farm was to go contracting, foot-paring sheep. I advertised for work, and everyone who had sheep too rough to handle or too difficult to treat rang up. The established foot-paring foot-rotters wouldn't handle these sheep and the owners couldn't, so I accepted these jobs as I didn't have much choice.

I employed a couple of strong young men, set up my sheep-handler, and with Kate and a new pup, Bedee, onboard, we left for our first job. Kate had shown much improvement and an immediate grasp of her duty only three weeks after that first-day lesson. Kate and I drafted 300 sheep without any assistance from any human. A neighbour and friend who sometimes lent me his good dog saw Kate in action and was quite put out that Kate was turning out so well so quickly.

Bedee was a mistreated and cringing black bitch that I had rescued. After Kate, Bedee was a disaster. She wouldn't come when you called her and she just ran straight at the sheep, scattering them in all directions. But after sleeping inside for a couple of weeks and eating regular meals, she began to come when called and do simple things like sit down, come behind, get off the chair, and things like that. I let her out with the sheep to see what would happen and she killed the first of three sheep by chasing a crazy weaner into a strainer post. She killed two more in similar fashion before she became Kate's well-behaved apprentice.

So, with two young, inexperienced men, two inexperienced dogs and being a bloke who is getting a bit old for this sort of caper, we arrived at our first foot-paring job. Shock one was, they weren't sheep but long-horn goats, big and tough, moving restlessly around this high-fenced sheep pen. We discussed the situation and decided we needed the work, so we set up our handling machine.

One of the workers provided shock number two. These were feral goats captured at Wilcannia, and they had never been handled. Our special race would have been useless, so we set up the machine against the permanent pen. The worker said his job was to keep them up into the handler for us all day. We were ready to go.

I took Kate and went to help the workers move the goats forward. 'Get over,' I said to Kate.

'Stop!' the worker yelled. 'They killed the boss's good dog this morning.'

I yelled to Kate but she was already around them. One goat charged her but somehow she got out of the way. I got in the pen and a goat charged me. I ducked. The worker wasn't so quick and the goat crashed into his shoulder and broke his collarbone. I dragged him to the side of the pen as goats charged and leapt high all around us.

'Get me out before we're killed,' he yelled as we dragged him over the fence and put him in the car. The boss arrived.

'Haven't you bastards handled goats before?' he said.

'Not wild ones like these,' we said.

He asked us who was going to pen them up because the injured worker was the only one who would do it. Then he looked into the pen and asked what was going on.

Kate hadn't got out of the pen as we thought but had gone around and around and had the goats circling in the big pen. I was surprised but pretended I knew she could do it. Trying to impress the boss to gain future work, I said I'd pen them up.

Kate worked all day and the boys cursed and swore, and the boss worked all day in my place on the machine, so pleased that at last he had found someone that could handle wild goats. When the goats got their wide horns stuck in the machine another worker ran in with a saw and cut the horns off, and as they tried to pull away Kate nipped-them on the legs to keep them up. The day was hot and dust swirled continually. At

162

afternoon smoko Kate couldn't jump the fence out of the pen to have a break because she was so tired. She lay in the shade for the 20-minute break and I lifted her back in for the last two-hour run.

Kate had handled the goats, wild as they were, so well at her first attempt that I eventually told the boss she hadn't seen goats before. He replied that I wasn't a bad worker but it was a pity I talked so much rubbish. Kate was lifted out of the pen and lay down in the most privileged position possible—in the twin cab ute—for the trip home. Despite the two boys' bruising and aches, they patted and wiped Kate down with a damp cloth for the duration of the 30-kilometre trip home.

Next day the word had got around the goat farm's neighbours that a bloke had a pretty good dog that could handle goats, so a few people wandered in during the day to see her work. From that job, people started to ring more frequently with offers of work.

The next job was a relief for everyone—1,500 head of Suffolk ewes needing a manicure. We set up the machine with our specially designed twin race so that sheep walked up to the machine side by side. They went into a single race at the end as they climbed up into the handling machine. The trick is to keep both sides of the race full all the time and if this is done efficiently, the sheep will run and enter the race a lot more easily, causing less stress on the sheep and the workers.

Bedee was about to get her first turn as she hadn't been allowed near the goats, or there would have been a substantial grave for dead goats if not some persons as well.

Kate, I must point out, had never seen the twin race system work before, nor had Bedee. So two boys worked on the machine as I was going to work with the dogs to teach them what to do. We filled the race and work started. As each race emptied I would walk up the side, push the stragglers up the front and then fill the race with more sheep. Soon Kate and Bedee both started pushing the sheep up the race on one side and I would get the other. I decided to make Kate stay on one side and get Bedee to work the other.

By 11.00 am on the first morning, the dogs knew what they had to do. Bedee would come around Kate's side and Kate would snap at her, nipping her to send her back. If they were filling the pen and Bedee stood in the wrong spot Kate would go up and snap at her, biting her sometimes, until she stood in the right position. After several jobs and two weeks, the dogs had become as professional as one could believe.

We started work at 7.30 am and stopped for 30 minutes at 9.30 am, and then worked through until noon, breaking up the afternoon in the same manner. We were working in 40 degree temperatures in the Riverina, and the only way to survive was to pace yourself correctly. The dogs learned the work schedule fast. If we called 'smoko', the dogs would stop work halfway through a bark to go and have a cold drink and lie in the shade, until time was up to start work again. We carried iced water for the dogs to drink and we always put it out for them. It turned out they wouldn't drink water, no matter how thirsty, unless we put it down for them.

Some time passed and the reputation of the dogs seemed always to proceed us.

For one job, we arrived at the property of a very big sheep dealer, a noted dog trainer, animal lover and, in general, a great bloke. Coincidentally, the person that gave me Bedee was shearing on the property with his four-man crew, so the place was a hive of activity. Since the shearers worked the same times as we did, the bloke that gave me Bedee didn't get a chance to see her work, but listened with increasing interest as the owner of the property related some of the skills of the two dogs.

On the first day we were there, the owner told me I would ruin the dogs as I used to pick them up and pat them and make a big fuss of them after any particular job they did. The boys also patted the dogs and made a fuss of them. The dog-trainer owner explained that dogs that work hard can't be handled like this as they become too spoilt and soft and won't work. However, after working on this property for two weeks we noticed he was putting his young dog in the front of the ute instead of the back, and he was also picking it up and patting it.

The owner's father had a champion dog that people talked about. He came over quietly one day and said he had to move some very valuable stud ewes and lambs. He wondered if I could lend him Kate. I said I had to come too as Kate would not work for anyone else, not even for the boys with me on the machine. He was very happy with Kate's effort and said if I was taking orders for pups, could I put his name down and he would pay me immediately.

Catch me if you can! My cattle dogs love to chase sticks and swim in the river and dams, but the red dog is always faster and more nimble than the blue dog. This photo says it all! **Mandy Archibald, Murrurundi, NSW**

All the sheep had been shorn and only the wild rams remained unpenned. The owner's dog had been run over six months previously by a car, and his young dog was too inexperienced for the job, so the shearers and other helpers came out to pen up the rams. The father's dog and one of the shearers' dogs wouldn't go in the pen, so I told my dogs to hop over. Kate got in the pen and got behind a gate as a ram charged her. Bedee went after the ram and they started to turn the rams around and around like the goats until they eventually went up the race. The chap who gave me Bedee called out that he had only been joking when he said I could have the dog. The shearers stopped for fifteen minutes just to watch them work.

The job was finished after almost three weeks, and the owner came down with a cheque and paid me for the job. I thanked him and then he handed me a cheque for $2,000 to cash at the bank in the local town. I was a bit confused because he had paid full price plus a bit extra for the job. He said, 'Cash that cheque on your way through town and leave Kate with me. She will have a good home.' No way, but thanks anyway.

Another time, we went to a place near Oaklands to do a job, one of the worst ever. We had to remove the dags, dried and large and copious enough to fill a plastic bucket, from every sheep. We battled along for days, with one of the boys quitting the job. However, a highlight was the farmer who had a dog that no-one could better. Talk about smart, this one was super-smart. He was so good he only went to work when he believed no-one else could do the job. He was big, same colour as Kate, black and tan, but heavier and about three-quarters the size of an Alsatian.

One of the many clever things he did was to run up alongside an escaping sheep, grab it by the wool on its shoulder and hold it until a human walked up and took the sheep from him. Bedee watched this with interest and ran out from her duties to inspect the technique more closely.

At the very next job we were doing, a sheep jumped the race and ran away. Bedee went after the sheep, grabbed it by the wool on its shoulder and held it until one of us came to take the sheep. From then on I called 'catch' to Bedee if I wanted a sheep caught in the paddock. Kate looked on each time. One day I was moving ewes and lambs with Kate on her own. I called out 'catch', forgetting Bedee was not there. Kate ran up behind the sheep I'd singled out, grabbed it by the back leg, flipped it over and held it until I came up.

When fly time was prevalent we took the gear to the paddock, circled the sheep, and I would point out a suspect fly-strike, call out 'catch', and one or two dogs would catch the sheep. They caught on so fast that, after we'd done this a couple of times, they didn't need to be told—as soon as we put the fly-strike equipment in the ute to drive to the paddock, the dogs would round up the sheep into a circle, find any fly-struck sheep themselves, and catch and hold them until we were ready.

They had become so skilled at every aspect of sheep handling that I took them for granted, talked to them like humans, always let them ride in the front of the ute—and they even slept inside the house—without ever a blemish to their great record.

People came and stood and looked in awe as the dogs continued to perform their duties with ever increasing skills. Once I had to move 3,000 head back home—a trek of about five miles. We set the sheep on the way, left the dogs with them, and I went home to do some other jobs.

The neighbour who'd laughed at Kate the day she came home called in and told me to keep an eye on my sheep because a big mob was coming down the road and no-one was with them.

'Hell, what happened to my dogs?' I said in panic. But the dogs were there and the neighbour couldn't believe his eyes that the young dog, who only a year or so earlier didn't know the meaning of 'way back', could move 3,000 sheep down the road efficiently.

The battle to keep the farm was eventually lost, and I now drive a truck for a living. Kate and Bedee take turn about to ride with me in the truck. No more sheep to work, no more applause from the crowd, no more excitement and challenge to do the impossible, but somehow the dogs seem to be happy to be with me—although sometimes I think they look and feel sorry for me because I no longer have the sheep to work nor do the jobs we loved doing.

Eric and the dogs keeping an eye on the weaners at Manbulloo Station, NT. **Mark Buttenshaw, West Wyalong, NSW**

A 'Northern Territory kelpie'

Geoffrey Blight Narrogin, WA

Annie was the first dingo I owned. She came from Central Australia via a truck driver who dropped her off at a friend's wildlife park.

As she crossed the West Australian border she had to become a 'Northern Territory kelpie' in order to get around State laws which attempt to prevent ownership of a dingo or dingo cross dog. Bureaucracy ignores the fact that a large percentage of working dogs in Australia are already dingo crosses.

I had tried to find books or information that could tell me more about dingoes, but nowhere was there anything about the possibility of dingoes making working sheepdogs. I had heard stories and spoken to men who said they had owned dingoes or dingo crosses. In the end I decided to get myself a dingo and test out my own theories.

I noticed immediately that there were many clear similarities between my kelpies and Annie. So I started training her as a sheepdog. She was friendly, very attractive and intelligent.

She proved all my suspicions—especially with her ability to read my thoughts. She wasn't as good as the sheepdogs I had—no doubt because they came from 400 years of rigorous selection—but to me there was no question that these dogs were very much a part of the kelpie history.

She often gave me heart attacks when she took things into her own hands. I became very wary of using her in public. Although she worked sheep, she did bite sometimes and I would have to discipline her. She was also very good at climbing out of her pen.

I had to attend my mother's funeral some 250 kilometres away. I was upset and impatient to leave when I noticed her standing in the paddock over the road from my house. When I tried calling her, she wouldn't come. I got angry and went after her, only to find she kept retreating across the paddock.

I couldn't get near her. I went back home and released some of her sheepdog mates for a run, thinking she would join them. The little rotter didn't. She just stayed over the road and continued to retreat if I approached, or came back toward me if I turned to walk home. I was getting very annoyed. I had to leave and no way was I going to leave her loose with no-one around for two days.

So I got the ute and went after her but she even outran that. Halfway across the paddock I realised she was going to beat me to the next paddock. This wasn't mine, so I stopped and returned home . . . for the rifle. It seemed the stories I had heard about dingoes going wild might indeed be true. I had never had this kind of trouble with her before. I certainly didn't want to shoot her, but I was running late and out of ideas. When I returned with the rifle she was back near the ute. I approached and she took off down the exact same line she'd followed each time before.

I jumped into the ute and pursued as fast as the paddock's rough surface would allow, noticing that she was occasionally looking back to see where I was. There was a small group of trees in the far corner and she was heading for it, flat-out. I thought she would just jump through the fence and keep going, and I tried to get the rifle ready to get a shot.

Suddenly, without warning, as she reached the trees she stopped, turned and sat. I couldn't believe it. As I drove right up to her, I could see her lip curling, which was her way of talking to me.

What was even more surprising, right beside her, jammed between two small trees, was a woolly hogget. It couldn't get out. I don't know whether Annie had chased it in there or what had happened, but it was unharmed and I let it go. Meanwhile Annie had jumped up on the ute and was ready for a lift home. I suddenly realised how close I had come to shooting her, believing she had gone wild.

I have seen several films and read the stories of dogs that wanted to tell their owners something important. Even after 40 years of working nearly every day with dogs, I had thought many such stories were mostly fictional. However, on that day, a very sad one due to the loss of Mum, I was confronted with evidence I can never dismiss. A plain ordinary desert dingo went to quite a deal of trouble—and risk—to attract me to something it felt I should know about.

After helping muster the cattle back into the paddock after a long day of branding and cutting calves, Pipa the blue cattle dog cools off in the little water which is left. Still alert and watching, she waits for directions to move in on the passing cattle and push them ahead. **Lauren Wilson, Allora, Qld**

Here's a picture of my dogs, Rusty (red and white), Denny (red and tan) and Gypsy (black and tan), cooling off after working on my grandparents' farm at Rutherglen. My dogs and I are townies during the week but we like to go out on weekends and work stock, be it at a trial or just poking around on a friend's farm. I got the two red dogs as pups from the Animal Aid shelter in Coldstream, so I got lucky that they both love to work and have won or been placed in cattle, sheep and duck trials. Denny has great poise and balance when working stock, and a natural ability to work out what you are trying to do, and help without any fuss or commands. Rusty is getting older and still enjoys working but has decided at times that she knows best, so if you give her a command there's every chance she'll just stop working and jump into the ute. Gypsy had all the right attributes to really make it as a great dog but is sadly no longer with us. It's only when you look back on their lives that you realise all the things the dogs have done that have resulted in laughter, frustration and celebration—too numerous to write down, and you have to keep some good stories to yourself. **Daniel Ball, Mount Evelyn, Vic**

'Hey city dog, can I get you a stool?' **Glenys Tranter, Woodberry, NSW**

Red Ted alert

Bruce Rodgers Yeelanna, SA

When I came to this district sixty-three years ago, my nearest neighbour, Mick Wagner, had a sheepdog called Red Ted. He was from a red kelpie bitch by a border collie dog. Ted was a good all-round sheepdog and had a lot of intelligence in matters other than working sheep.

We had a scrub block which had no improvements adjoining the Wagner farm. So we were using Wagner's stable and horse yards, and camped in a hut near the sheds.

One night about midnight, Ted insisted on barking at Mick's back door and would not stop when told. Then he went to the bedroom window and put his paws on the sill and barked more than ever.

Mick got out of bed and, armed with a hurricane lantern, went to investigate. The first thing he saw was his own two horses in the back garden, and he realised that our eight horses would not be far away. He found them beginning to tear open and eat some seed wheat which had been pickled and stacked in bags. Fortunately they had not eaten much, because a big dose of pickled wheat would have killed them. Horses at that time were scarce and precious.

My father said Ted was an exceptional and very valuable dog. He had probably saved us a small fortune in having to replace our horses if they had died. We made sure the horse yards gate was closed correctly thereafter.

Elevated to the peerage

Jim Kelly Naracoorte, SA

Our Prince Charles arrived on the same day in 1948 as his royal namesake. He was a fat and cuddly red kelpie pup with possibly a drop or two of dingo blood. If Charlie wasn't the pick of the litter, somebody else got an exceptional choice.

He learnt his name very quickly and was one of those amazing pups who seemed to know all he had to, right from the start. Except for the occasional ride in the old army surplus jeep, dogs had to do all their own footwork in those days. We always carried a stockwhip and galloped about a lot more than we do today. The young dog had no fear of the whip and seemed to develop a special relationship with Solo and Melody, the main stockhorses in our stable. On hot days, while our horses were tied up to the fence, he would stand in the horses' shadows, where the ground was cooler. In the middle of the day, this often meant lying under the tail of the horse, right next to the potentially dangerous back hoofs.

As time went by, Charlie developed into the most outstanding dog of my life, both as a yard dog and as a paddock worker, with a big wide cast. He was a rarity in this age of specialisation of eye, bark and cast. He would work for any one of the family and as he grew older, was rarely tied up. We loved him with respect and admiration.

In the middle of the night in August 1955, when we had a team of Poll Shorthorn bulls on feed in the bull pens, I was awakened by Charlie barking at my bedroom window on the front verandah. We had a baby daughter in an adjoining room and were frightened the hullabaloo would wake up the rest of the household. I told Charlie in my gruffest, deepest, whisper to 'Go and lie down.'

To our surprise, he barked back. I said, 'Something must be wrong, he's trying to tell me something,' and leapt out of bed into a dressing gown. With a torch from the kitchen, I left the house by the back door. Charlie met me with a wagging tail as we walked down the path to the bull shed. As we got closer,

I could hear banging, crashing and very heavy breathing. A gate had come open somehow and two bulls were fighting in a confined space. It was tricky and dangerous separating such big, angry animals. Charlie barked and distracted them long enough for me to push one through the gate and close the catch.

Prince Charles was a hero. The bruises to the bulls must have been superficial, as they won big ribbons at the Royal Adelaide Show a few weeks later.

I've spent my working life of some fifty years with animals. I've seen some remarkable behaviour where an individual has performed in special ways, either to solve a problem or bring attention to themselves, but always within the normal range of behaviour for its species. A cow that hides her calf, a draught horse that pulls to the utmost of its strength, a sheep which always walks through a gate first so the mob follows.

They are displays of superior intelligence that make close contact with individual animals such a rewarding experience. But Charlie's behaviour that night was quite exceptional, outside the norm, even for a smart dog.

Consider his position. Somehow he became aware of the commotion going on in the bull shed. Perhaps he slept there, we don't know. Normal dog behaviour would have been to bark at the fighting bulls till something happened.

Charlie knew he could not fix the problem and must have known I could. When I scolded him for barking at the window, normal behaviour would have been to lower his tail and head and skulk away, yet he kept barking in a most defiant and unusual way, so that I got the message that he needed help. He kept the idea to deliver the message in his head, despite the scolding.

For me this was a unique experience that I have often contemplated. Down our way Charlie was elevated to the peerage despite his colonial background. We addressed him from time to time as Sir Charles.

My partner and I are furniture removalists. On one of our trips West we stopped at our regular truck stop at Cooma. It was full of cattle trucks from the stock sales earlier that day. We found a spot next to a cattle truck. I looked to see if there were any animals, and was greeted by a kelpie. He had a great big smile and looked straight at me. I looked closer and saw there were actually three dogs, with a kennel right at the bottom of the truck. The truck door opened and out came a young truckie. As soon as the dogs heard him they got excited and ran up and down, pacing the truck. He gave them a quick look before hopping back into the truck and driving off. I showed my partner the photo and said, 'If only we had workers as happy, excited and hardworking as those dogs!' I decided to give a copy of the photo to the dog's owner, if I ever met him. Anyway, weeks later, after I'd got the photo printed, we stopped at the truck stop. The place was full of truckies having their lunch. I got my partner to show one of the truckies the photo, hoping he'd know whose dog it was. To my surprise he did, and pointed to the young fellow behind him, who said that his dog's name was Nudge and that on the day I took the photo it was Nudge's first birthday and that he was a 'keeper', meaning that he was turning out to be a good working dog. **Ingrid Stevens, Merimbula, NSW**

Old Don of St Kilda

Beryl Thomas Toowoomba, Qld

My childhood was spent on St Kilda, my parents' property twenty miles north of Roma in western Queensland. Sheepdogs were part of our life. They lived in kennels under the pepper trees, chained up when they weren't working in the paddocks or the sheepyards. They were kelpie–collie crosses mostly, some red, some black and white, some a mixture, with names like Snip and Don and Treacle, Lassie and Laddie. The dogs changed but the names were recycled.

Old Don was one of the red ones. At that time, in the early 1940s, my father rode a horse called Derry, a big chestnut. Don always trotted alongside. The three of them were very much a team. If Don was very tired or the burrs bad, he would be taken up on the pommel of the saddle—there were no motorbikes then.

On this particular day, my father went off in the morning with Derry and Don to check the dams. He rode past the windmill and the wool-shed and my mother waved to him from the verandah of the house. We children were all away then—one brother in the RAAF and my other two brothers and I were at boarding schools near the coast. It was a lonely life for my mother and a busy time for my father because of course during wartime there was little extra help available.

Mother used to write all the news from home in letters describing everything in detail for us. The events of this day—a day we still discuss at family reunions—were recorded with special care and have been repeated often, because this is the day Old Don became a hero.

Dad always came home for a hot dinner in the middle of the day, but he was sometimes held up, so my mother was not unduly concerned by his lateness that day. She was surprised, though, when Old Don came home by himself and barked at the bottom of the back steps. An occasional dog was sent home in disgrace, but never Old Don. He stayed close by my mother, whimpering and barking.

Clearly, all was not well. Although my mother had driven a sulky as a country schoolteacher and as a young wife, in all her 90 years she never did learn to drive a car. She called the nearest neighbour on the phone, a party line with five families connected. The neighbour was over in half an hour with his widowed mother, who had been a nurse. They drove out across the paddocks following Don, who led them to my father, lying injured and in great pain in a steep gully.

Derry had tripped and fallen forward as he was going up the side of the gully and Dad's foot had been caught between the stirrup and the bank. Many bones in his foot and leg had been broken when the horse had struggled free and scrambled out of the gully. Derry was lame, but he set out for home and arrived very late that day. Don was determined to stay with my father. Apparently it had taken some persuading by my father to convince Don to leave him and go home, but persuade him he did and off Don had gone, as fast as he could, straight to my mother. Had he not done this, a search party would have had enormous difficulty locating my father—it may have taken days.

My father recovered and went on riding horses and working sheepdogs for a long time after that. He lived to be ninety-one.

Family with 'all hands on board' for a day's cattle work. **Judy Winfield, Beaudesert, Qld**

This trucking life

Neil Macpherson Tamworth, NSW

I had got myself a new truck in 1965 and went stock carrying, something I had always wanted to do. A chap from Bendemeer gave me a small red kelpie pup. I liked the small breed of kelpie because, as truck dogs, they could manoeuvre around the pens and run in under the sheep easily. This pup's brother and sister had been sold for high prices and finished up in New Zealand. So I had high hopes for Sandy, as I called him. As time went on, I was proved correct.

Sandy was put in that new truck when he was six weeks old. He sat or lay on the floor and later, when he got a bit older, he sat on the passenger's side which I had covered with a blanket. In those days heating wasn't considered necessary in a truck, but one dog was as good as a heater. Sandy travelled in that truck for five and a half years and was never sick or smelly. Mind you, every time I got out, so did my dog.

I needed to spend every Monday at the Tamworth saleyards, where about 10,000 sheep and lambs went through each time. Among other jobs, I would cart about six or seven loads of sheep to the abattoirs. Sandy and I could load these with the minimum of work and trouble. He was an outstanding truck dog. I would leave the side window down when I arrived at the saleyards and Sandy would stay in the truck until I gave him his special whistle. Although there would be 100 trucks and about 200 dogs and all the noise of the sheep, gates banging and men shouting, he would somehow find me.

One day Sandy didn't answer my call, so I asked around: 'Have you seen my little red dog?' Everyone knew him but nobody had seen him that day. After some time, maybe two hours, I was convinced he had jumped into some other red truck and that I wouldn't see him again. The next thing, along came Sandy, full of apologies and very wet and tonguing. He had just had a cool-off in the trough. Mick Pullman, one of Jack Smyth's right-hand men, came hobbling after the dog and said to me, 'Thanks for the loan of your dog, Mac. He is a real little beauty. He and I have just drafted 2,000 sheep on our own.' That was high praise indeed, because Jack Smyth was second only to Sir Sid Kidman as a cattle dealer and dealt in hundreds of thousands of sheep, so Mick would have seen a lot of dogs in his time.

But thanks a lot, indeed, Mick. Despite the flattery, my dog had done a day's work for someone else and I still had six or seven loads of sheep to put on my own truck. Nevertheless, I was proud of my dog, but he was pretty tired that night.

Sandy was never tied up in later life. He always slept near that truck and everywhere the truck went, so did Sandy—even carting wheat from local farms into the silos in Tamworth.

When eventually I sold the truck and business, the buyer turned to me after he had given me the cheque. 'Righto, Mac,' he said, 'how much do you want for the little red dog?'

I was moving to town and town life is no life for a dog, let alone a working sheepdog, so I informed the new truck owner that he didn't have enough money in the bank to buy Sandy. But if he promised to give him a good life and let him ride in his truck, then he could have him for nothing.

I saw that dog ten years later when he was very old. He answered me when I called him and we had a bit of a cuddle-up. He was happy.

Queens of the road

Fred Eldering Crookwell, NSW

I was returning home after a sheep show around midnight, towing the canvas-covered trailer behind my ute. Beside me, stretched out on the seat with her head resting on my leg, was my old border collie bitch, Stardy—still travelling after eighteen years, mother of many champions and veteran of many sheepdog exhibitions and trials.

Since 1947, a Stardy had always been on the front seat of the truck or ute with me, keeping me company during the long, lonely hours on the road trucking cattle and sheep. They all carried the stud names of Greyleigh Stardust, but the Stardy on my seat that night was the last of the original strain that had formed the basis of my stud, the oldest registered working border collie stud in Australia, founded in 1947.

The lights of the ute shone down the highway and I fondled the old girl's ear and smiled. Coming up behind me, I could see in the side mirror the fairyland lights of a big rig. I pulled down the mike of the CB: 'You're clear, mate,' I told him. The rig passed and pulled over to the left with words of thanks from the driver.

The CB crackled again. 'That you, old Freddie?' the driver said. It was an old mate, Mac. So as the kilometres rolled by, the two of us, whose paths had not crossed for a few years, chatted on.

'I don't suppose old Stardy is still on the seat beside you, Freddy?' he said. 'She would have passed on by now. I would sure like a quid for every mile she's shared in the cab with you.'

Back went my reply that she was indeed sleeping in her usual place. We both swung off the highway and drew up in the parking area of a truck stop. The rig driver came over and we greeted each other warmly, then he gently lifted the old dog from the seat and hugged her before placing her on the ground for her wee break.

Inside the truck stop, the woman on duty insisted on taking 'the offsider', old Stardy, her usual two sausages—before she even got our black coffees. We settled down for a bit of a chat and, seeing the fuss that everyone had made over my old dog, I told Mac the story about how I had got a replacement for old Stardy, for the time when she would no longer be with me in the cabin.

About eight months earlier, Stardy had picked up a virus and was very sick. The vet had advised putting her down, but I took her home, treated her and nursed her through her illness. One day when she looked like she was never going to get back on her feet, I whispered to her to hang on. 'I don't want to lose you yet, old girl,' I told her. 'Who will be my truck dog? I've got no-one to take your place.'

Extraordinarily, some weeks later my top breeding bitch, who was then twelve years old and had not been in season for over three years, came on heat and mated with a young dog I had. She never looked pregnant at any time, yet presented me with two beautiful pups and reared them well. In all my years of breeding dogs, I had never seen an old bitch come on heat after such a break.

When the pups were ten days old, I was looking at them when the old girl walked in. 'Mac, you know how the old girl is with pups that are not hers once they are three weeks old?' I said. 'She savages them.'

'Well, I picked up the bitch pup, showed it to her and told her to look after her as she was my next truck dog. She nuzzled the pup, put her head under my arm and looked up as if to say, "I understand boss".

'From the time the pup was a month old, she shared the old girl's mattress, sleeping between her legs and sharing her feed.

My grandson Euan and I were visiting relatives on a sheep property in Kotupna, Northern Victoria. This was a new experience for Euan and, as a treat, the farmer let him help with the mustering of the sheep with the working dogs. When it was finished one of the dogs who'd taken a liking to Euan jumped up into the back of the farmer's ute with him. **Mike Clements, Frenchs Forest, NSW**

Old Stardy never once snapped or snarled at the pup, the way she does with all the other youngsters. When the pup was old enough, Stardy allowed her the privilege of sharing her rug on the front seat of the ute—a thing that was taboo to all other dogs. She had never let another dog into the front of the ute or truck before.

'The pup is now four months old. The old girl has taught her how to behave in the cab—a quick snarl usually pulls her into line. The only reason the pup is not with Stardy and me tonight is that I have been away for a few days and my grand-daughter insisted the pup stayed with her.

'So, Mac, although I thought I knew animals, I cannot explain how it is that both bitches seemed to work together to produce a new truck dog for me. It was as if they knew of the big hole there would be in my life with the loss, eventually, of the old girl.'

We parted after we had finished our meal, but not before Mac had opened the door of the ute and fondled the old dog's head. 'See you, old girl. If not, thanks for the memories.'

Stardy lived on for another year and was nineteen when she died. The new truck dog carries the name of Little Stardy, but we also know her as The Miracle, because that's what we reckon she is.

I am nearly 70 now, but I still do sheepdog exhibitions in Sydney at the Castle Hill Show, and Little Stardy is one of my stars. I also give overseas visitors at conferences a look at how our dogs work. One of my recent escapades was to drive some sheep into the Regent Hotel in Sydney, put them into the lift, then shepherd them among the tables in the dining room where the delegates were enjoying dinner. That went down really well!

In 1979 and 1981 I won the Australian Championships at Mudgee with Greyleigh Mist and Greyleigh Snoopy—but I still reckon the way my old dogs produced a truck dog for me was one of the really special things that has happened in my life.

177

Searching for his truck

Stephen Foott Swan Hill, Vic

The following is the true story of Butch, lost from a stock crate at Tailem Bend at two o'clock one Friday morning.

Unaware that Butch had climbed through the bars of the crate, the driver returned to Swan Hill. All hell broke loose when it was discovered Butch was missing as he was a third-generation truck and paddock dog.

I rang my brother, Peter Foott, who was working in Adelaide at the time. A day later Peter located Butch in the caravan park at Tailem Bend. Happy to be amongst friends again, Butch took up residence with Peter's family at Marleston, which is close to Adelaide airport.

But Butch was terrified of the sound of the jets taking off and landing. Returning home from work two days later, Peter discovered Butch had jumped over a six-foot galvanised iron fence and had disappeared. Peter rang the RSPCA and reported Butch missing. A search began and two hours later Butch was located ten miles from Peter's home, sitting in front of a service station apparently waiting for 'his' truck to come along.

After work one week later, Peter discovered Butch was gone again. This time he had chewed his way through a flyscreen, got into the flat, smashed another flyscreen and escaped. Both windows had been open at the time. Peter rang the RSPCA, reported Butch missing and returned to Swan Hill for the long weekend. Sadness and disappointment prevailed and we gave up Butch as lost forever.

On his return to Adelaide, Peter once more rang the RSPCA. A terrified Butch had indeed been sighted running through the Adelaide traffic, but no-one had been able to apprehend him.

To Peter's amazement, three days later the RSPCA rang to inform him that Butch had turned up at the Noarlunga Abattoir, 27 miles from Adelaide. It was a location he had been to only three times. The last time had been two weeks previously, and wasn't via Adelaide, but over the punt at Wellington.

The drover at the abattoir had come to work early in the morning and found this red dog, very tired and footsore, at the gate. Immediately the gates were opened, the dog had run to the truck ramps. The drover realised the dog was lost and rang the RSPCA.

Since his experiences in metropolitan Adelaide, Butch makes sure he never gets left behind again. He now plants himself beside the right-hand-side wheel of the truck after it's unloaded.

While Bill Walker and his brother Richard own a cropping and sheep property in the wheat belt of WA, it is Hunter who reigns supreme as farm boss! A five-year-old huntaway-kelpie, Hunter is a loyal companion, much loved pet and highly valued working dog. His cheerful, friendly temperament and enthusiasm in the sheep yard, paddock and shearing shed have made him popular with all. He greets shearers, stockmen, truck drivers, farmers and visitors from the city as if they are his best friend. His bark is one of authority but it is rarely heard when he is not taking charge and supervising the workplace. For relaxation after a long day's work he enjoys evening walks with his owners, and never backs down from the opportunity to chase rabbits and foxes. While he enjoys swimming in dams and freshwater soaks, Hunter is not fond of the occasional soapy wash. **Marie Walker, Quairading, WA**

A dedicated partner

Geoffrey Blight Narrogin, WA

It was spring in the worst year of my life. I was broke. Sharefarming wheat was going very poorly and we were involved in a legal wrangle over the land and the house we lived in. My wife was pregnant with our first child, so I was glad to get some crutching on a local farm about nineteen miles away.

It was a small place, only one stand in the shearing shed, an old house, an old man and an old blue dog.

There weren't many sheep, about 1,100 all told, which needed crutching and then they were to be sold. The farm had already been sold and the old man was moving into a home in Perth. He had no family, just his dog Scotty and he was to be put down when the sheep were gone.

Scotty couldn't go to the new home—they wouldn't allow it, and he did have trouble with his bowels and smelt quite often after some young fellow had run over him near the shed.

The shearing shed was very old and flimsy. A stiff breeze could have demolished it. The shed held only about 50 sheep in just two pens separated by a picket garden gate. As I kicked off, the old man explained his predicament and also asked if I'd mind, each time I finished a pen, throwing the picket gate open so the still unseen dog could do the penning up.

Well I had heard a few stories, and I had been shearing for a few years and seen a fair bit of action, but I guess I didn't believe any dog was going to do what the old man reckoned. Still, he was a nice old fellow so I thought, if I had to, I wouldn't mind penning for myself. I'd had it worse. As the old chap wasn't able to stay for some reason or other, when I had finished the first pen, I did what he said and opened the back gate. But I still couldn't see the dog.

I reckoned it was taking me about one and a quarter minutes to crutch each sheep. When I straightened up and saw the pen full, I received a shock as I had not heard any noise through the closed gate in the front wall of the pen.

When the second pen was done I repeated the exercise. Same result. I could hardly believe it. When I had the chance I directed

180

a few how-are-you-mates to the bent old blue dog I fleetingly caught sight of. He showed no interest in me whatsoever, even seemed suspicious of me, so I didn't push my luck.

The crutching lasted three days and was a piece of cake. The old dog had those sheep so well trained they penned more like milking cows than wild wheatbelt sheep.

I guess it was my praise for the old dog that made the old man ask if I would like old Scotty. He assured me that, although he could not run, he would still pull his weight for a while yet and as long as I didn't take him into the house, the smell wasn't too bad. He had visibly shown he wasn't looking forward to putting his dog down and no-one else wanted him. I thought he probably didn't know many people that well, having lived a very secluded life. The whole area had only recently seen extensive clearing, except for a few scattered properties, including his, that were the remnants of an attempt in the thirties to open up the land.

A few weeks later the old man phoned and said it was time to come and take Scotty. He had to leave the next day. Scotty now was mine—but only till the next morning. By then, he was gone. I found him back at the now empty old house, looking pretty weary. That didn't stop him biting me as I tried and finally succeeded in pushing him into the car.

Next morning, I found he had slipped the collar and was gone again. I cursed him and swore he could go to hell.

After three days I relented. I took the gun and went back to the old man's former home, quite prepared to put him down rather than leave him to starve. He looked very old and hungry and surprised me by rising from where he had been sitting on the verandah and walking straight to the car, hopping in quite voluntarily.

Scotty didn't run away again but I didn't have much sheep work for him at that time so during the harvest, he just sat lazily around with our very useless Labrador. They both passed their time killing hundreds of mice that were in plague proportion everywhere.

The harvest was a failure. By Christmas it was clear we would have to get out and go back to the sheep country I'd come from and go back shearing again.

I had about 600 mixed sheep running over 5,000 acres of sparsely cleared land on the cropping block where we lived. These would have to be mustered, which would take many days as they had spread all over the place in small mobs.

The weather was stinking hot, over 120 degrees on the back verandah of the tin shed type residence we lived in. I had thought I could probably catch the sheep at the three water points, though that would take even longer, building yards and shutting two points off. They might not even travel to the third water point anyway.

I was surprised when, just as the sun broke on Boxing Day, I became aware that a lot of sheep were bunching over some spilt wheat not too far from the house. It was a marvellous opportunity to just round them up and into the one yard we had. I was on foot with just Scotty, because it was too rough for a vehicle in most places, and I hadn't caught the horse. I sent the dog, fully expecting him to just pull them in.

As I have said, Scotty couldn't run and I soon realised that the sheep were going to get away despite my urging and swearing. Eventually, I hurled a stick at the dog, who wasn't going any faster than I was, which sure wasn't fast enough. Out of sight they went and I gave it up as a bad job and forgot about them.

The day was a real scorcher and there was no getting away from the heat. By mid-afternoon, the wife and I had settled for lying under the fan on the bed. I was nearly asleep when I became aware that large amounts of dust were drifting into the house, but we couldn't hear any vehicles approaching.

Staggering out the open front door, I was in no way prepared for what I saw. I had forgotten about the sheep and Scotty a good ten hours ago. I could not believe it. Here was what looked like 600 sheep moving very, very quietly and slowly up to the house, followed by a staggering, old, blue dog.

Ewan Eatts and the farm dog, Pip. Pip is the boss on a cattle, sheep and orchard farm owned by Ewan's dad, Bevan, in Manjimup, WA. Most times when you enter a farm yard you'll meet the farm dog first, and it's usually a noisy occasion.
Craig Kinder, North Perth, WA

It was going to be a while before what had happened sank in. I swiftly took advantage of the muster and yarded them with total ease as the sheep seemed to quietly accept their capture. It was only when this was complete that I became concerned about the condition of Scotty—his staggering, his bleeding feet, his flanks tucked up and his fast and erratic panting. His eyes were sunken as he lay exhausted in the nearest shade.

In the next half hour I tried in vain to cool and calm and water him. It frightened me as he gulped and then shuddered in a fit as I withdrew the water. However, greater powers than either of us took a hand. While I watched, believing that Scotty was very close to death, the wind came fast, followed by black storm-clouds bearing wonderfully cooling drops of rain.

Although the storm was short, it seemed to have the right effect. The dog lay motionless on the verandah, his breathing calm, and he now seemed able to cope.

Because of the rain, I had some trouble tracking what exactly had happened. It became obvious the old dog had continued that morning in his pursuit of the sheep, managing to keep them grouped to a north boundary for miles, before they had been turned and gradually pushed back. At times they would have had to pass through scrub and regrowth which would have presented any dog with trouble. He had probably seen no water at all.

Being then young, it would take me some years to realise the significance of that muster. As I worked and trained dogs I came to understand the incredible dedication that can be counted on in a dog when he has spent a lifetime sharing the job as a sole partner to a human being.

182

Job's done, sheep are loaded, and it's time to head for the sale yards. They never leave without me. **Julie M Bennett, Stoneleigh, Vic**

It was love at first sight for Jock, our neighbour's sheepdog, and our little Sadie. Maybe the fact that both had been mistreated and were rescued drew them together. While Jock was a wonderful working dog, Sadie had nothing but play on her mind. They both loved riding together on the back seat of the quad bike, and the minute Sadie heard the bike coming down the road, she was there to catch a ride. Jock took on the hopeless task of teaching Sadie how to round up sheep. Sadie however, thought it was a great game Jock played and always messed things up for him. While everybody was highly amused about Sadie, Jock was the one who was told off for not doing his work properly. Jock was very patient with Sadie, but then one day, before he started to round up the sheep, he sat in front of her and just stared at her. A few seconds later, with her tail between her legs, Sadie turned around, sat on the sidelines and watched. After the sheep were secured, Peter, Jock's owner said: 'Good work, Jock, you can go now.' That was Jock's signal that his work was done. He ran over to Sadie and they both played together like little puppies. Today Sadie sits patiently on the sideline and waits for Jock until his work is done.

Vera Rayson, Campbell Town, Tas

A whirlwind at their heels

David Griffiths Port Lincoln, SA

Our in-town escape artist, Jilly, went to live on our friends' cattle property at Walcha to be trained to work, and soon captured the heart of their son. Jilly and Mark Junior became almost inseparable, and she was too busy doing what she was born to do to have time to think about running away! **Daneile Allen, Cootamundra, NSW**

When Mo first indicated his desire and ability to work in the sheep yards, I thought I had a freak. Then I discovered that Australian silky terriers descend from several original families, some of which were working stock. Mo proved that to be true.

During the latter years of my farming career, I owned three dogs—two paddock workers and the diminutive Mo. With a pedigree longer than him, he was eager to work and was afraid of nothing. During drafting, after every 50 or 60 sheep he would come through the race to be sure I was there—checking I was doing my job as he was doing his.

Woe betide any ewe that doubted his authority and hammered him against the fence. With teethmarks on her nose, she would have a whirlwind nipping at her heels in the best blue heeler tradition.

At the end of the job Mo, dirty and often bruised, would be carried to the house to be cleaned up and praised. He was the best yard dog I ever had.

Cheeky singer

Betty Draffen Macarthur, Vic

Cheeky, our kelpie cross, was unintentionally conditioned to sing a song on command.

Whenever my husband sharpened his combs and cutters on the grinder during shearing, the harsh sound aggravated the dog so much that he howled. Eventually he obliged with a 'song' without the accompanying noise of the grinder. All my husband had to say was, 'Sing a song, Cheeky,' and he would throw his head back and 'sing'.

One weekend Bill left Cheeky in the care of his shearers who were staying at the Jerilderie Hotel while he travelled home to Geelong for the weekend.

In the early hours of the morning the shearers stealthily took Cheeky up to their room and invited him to 'sing a song'. The idea was to disturb another group of shearers with whom they had a score to settle. Cheeky's soaring tenor voice disturbed them all right—as well as the publican.

I'm pleased to say it wasn't Cheeky who suffered any consequences.

186

Whoever said diamonds are a girl's best friend, never owned a dog. **Chloe Edwards, Pingelly, WA**

Gilbert inspects the camera. After a long drive from Calvert Hills Station in Cape York to Gillespie Station in Blackall, Central Queensland, Gilbert was keen for a run. This photo shows him post-run, tied up and waiting for a feed while Tommy unloads his swag in the background. **Alec 'Butch' Walker, Blackall, Qld**

Hoon driver

Barbara Shugg Stratford, Vic

We had heard of the oldest son borrowing Dad's car, and a younger son doing a bit of circle work around the front paddock, but were quite unprepared for the kelpie pup to take off in the farm ute.

It was towards the end of the '71 drought. The new black and tan was settling in nicely. He was showing plenty of eye and was very willing. The only command that he really understood, though, was 'sit'.

As was the daily procedure, the farm ute was loaded up with fifteen opened bags of oats. The young pup and the master climbed into the cabin and drove to the south paddock to feed the ewes.

The ute was put into low-range first gear and set in motion. The pup was left in the cabin while his master leapt onto the tray. Balanced precariously on the tail gate, he proceeded to trickle out the grain to the sheep, which were panicked into a feeding frenzy. The ute chugged slowly around the paddock for some distance and the frantic mob began to settle.

Suddenly, the motor roared. The vehicle bolted forward, sending the farmer flying off the back into the midst of his nervous sheep. The engine roared and the ute bumped across the paddock, bouncing in and out of potholes, scattering grain in all directions. The farmer and his sheep took off in hot pursuit.

The pup was of the 'when-in-doubt, sit' variety. The louder the boss yelled, the harder the confused pup sat on the accelerator, and the faster the ute bumped around the paddock, the more the bleating sheep chased after their food supply.

It wasn't until the farmer lost his voice that the pup ventured up onto the seat and peered out the window to see what was causing all the commotion. The boss, gasping gentle encouragement to the dog, finally managed to keep him off the floor long enough to catch his utility.

189

Amazing the uninitiated

Max Williams Exford, Vic

It was my daughter, with some of her first job money, who bought Ralph for me. I'd had dogs before, and good ones too—but Ralph was really something special.

A pedigree border collie, from trials and working dog parents, he soon showed he could carry on the tradition of his forebears. The breeder, Vern Sullivan, was keen to see new people doing the trials circuit, so he sent up a couple of his mates to encourage me. Soon, every spare moment, Ralph and I, and three sheep, sometimes more, would be out practising.

Now, this story isn't about Ralph's trials career, but his career does have a bearing on it. Rather, it is about what any sheepdog worth its salt does, and that's drafting sheep.

Our sheep agent came one morning to draft out some lambs from the ewes, a mob of about four hundred. As he was going on to a bigger job next, he had recruited a chap from the office to help for the day. This chap was a nice fellow, keen to get stuck into it, and had obviously seen somewhere that it was done by hopping into the pen, flapping your arms about, yelling 'Ho, ho, ho', and generally working up a sweat, while a kelpie springs on the sheeps' backs, barking furiously.

Well, we'd just started the job when, thinking to have a bit of fun, I said to this chap, 'No, we don't do it that way. Ralph is boss here. We'll just open and shut the gate for him.'

I could see he was a bit dubious, but I just opened the drafting pen gate, said to Ralph, 'Get over, Ralph,' and the yard was very quickly filled. Ralph then was in amongst them, pushing them through, no blocks and no barks, while we just chatted.

I could see the office chap was pretty impressed by this, so thought I would jazz the next scene up a bit. As soon as the drafting yard was empty, I opened the gate again, and Ralph filled it up as usual. But now I played my trump card. Just as I was shutting the gate, I looked at Ralph and said, 'Ralph, I think we can get a few more in here. Bring another three.'

Now, I knew from my trials training that Ralph loved working three sheep, and that my chances of him bringing that many from the mob were pretty good. Sure enough, back he came, three sheep in front, and straight into the pen. If the chap was impressed before, then this time he was goggle-eyed.

The mood had grabbed me by this time, so while Ralph was in the pen pushing, I was saying things like, 'Steady on, Ralph, that's Karen and she's made a nice job of that lamb,' or 'Get that one there, Ralph, she's always been a smarty.'

On the next few penfuls, it was much the same. If I said, 'Get three more,' and Ralph came back with more, I'd just cover up by saying, 'OK, if you think they'll fit. You're the boss!'

All that was a long time ago now, and the agent later said that the chap couldn't stop talking about it back at the office—about how Ralph could even count.

Ralph is retired now. He's sixteen years old and his daughter does the sheep work. Ralph likes going shopping these days, so he can have the donut my wife buys him. He also likes lying in the sun.

When I first got Ralph, I said to my trials mates, 'Well, at least I know a bit about sheep,' and, 'This is what I'm going to teach Ralph…' Both statements were pretty stupid. I had much to learn about sheep, and Ralph taught me more than I taught him.

I know Ralph's time is getting short now and that one day he won't be with us, But in another way, he will always be there—amazing the uninitiated with what a real working dog can do.

They say you don't choose a dog but a dog chooses you, and this was the case with Fergie. As a pup Fergie learnt how to climb out of the bitch box and follow me back to the house. As soon as I'd gone inside she'd run back and climb in with her mum, Miss. None of the other pups learnt how to do this. I've been blown away by Fergie's intelligence. When we are droving sheep along the road, she knows when to run around and head them into the gate. She loves riding on the motorbike and has to be the first to see anything, which is why she loves to get up high on the front of the bike. The worst part about this is, when she has found something dead to roll in, the smell is right in my face!
Ross and Sarah Thomson, Keeyuga Glenaroua via Kilmore, Vic

Gift takes on the job

Charles Vosper Gympie, Qld

The old dog was curled up in a ball. He was barely alive and shivering like hell. I don't mind telling you that tears came to my eyes when I saw him there. I knew old Darkie had moved his last cow in off the paddocks. As for the pup, Gift, I think he knew too, because he just lay there with his head resting on his front paws.

I told Peter about Darkie and he asked me to take him to the vet and have him put to sleep, but to bring him home and lay him to rest where he belongs. It was a chore I wasn't looking forward to, but it had to be done. After breakfast I found Gift was still there beside his old mate. He was a bit put out when I put Darkie in the truck.

That afternoon I let Gift off the chain, but he just didn't want to work. I had to get the herd in with some help from my wife. Gift had found the spot on the bank above the main yard where I had buried Darkie. He had a bit of a dig and sniff around but wouldn't come away and leave him. He stayed there for three days, as if he was waiting for Darkie to get up.

On the fourth day I went down to the milking shed and had switched the lights on and was putting the rinse water through the machines when I had this feeling that something was watching me. There, standing in the half light, was Gift. He was crawling along down low on his belly and sort of crying. I took his head in my hands and said to him, 'I know, mate. I miss him too.'

You know, if I didn't know better I would reckon that dog knew what I said, for he seemed to liven up a bit. I gave him the order to 'go forward' and away he went. From that day on he never looked back. It was a real treat to watch that young dog working. The old dog had surely done a good job as a teacher.

Drover (on the right) is an old dog now. He's blind and deaf, and awfully ugly. But his master loves him, and he was handy with the cattle in his younger days. He was accidently left in the stockyard by a droving mob, and found three days later, starving and with a broken leg. He must have used most of his nine lives by now. He's been attacked by another dog and left with gaping wounds. His master nearly put him out of his misery, but Drover sat up and looked at him. He could climb a pretty high fence despite that leg injury. Another time he was found by a neighbour in a yard of female kelpies. One hot month last year, he went missing for ten days. A neighbour four kilometres away found him in a gully with no water and unable to clamber out. Little Charlie (on the left) might be small, but he's as brazen as his larger mate.
Leonie Dettmann, Charters Towers, Qld

Teaching the apprentice a lesson

Neville Kajewski Emerald, Qld

My old friend Fred Wilson had a cattle dog called Ho, a wonderful worker and clever in many ways.

Ho wasn't just a good worker, he was Fred's mate and constant companion. I'm sure they knew each other's thoughts.

In the latter part of Ho's life, Fred bought a pup to train as a replacement before arthritis completely immobilised the old dog.

One day, Fred, Ho and the pup were yarding a mob of bullocks for dipping. According to established routine, once the mob was mustered Fred took the lead on his horse, allowing the dogs to bring them along while he opened the gates.

All was going well until a couple of bullocks decided they were going home. Under normal circumstances they would be no more than a nuisance to Ho. He would simply return them to the mob with a couple of disciplinary nips to nose and heel, but he hadn't reckoned on the inexperience of the pup.

When the two bullocks broke away, the rest of the mob turned. The pup, thinking he should be behind them, went to what was now the back of the mob.

Ho's barking at the two breakaways stirred the pup to enthusiastic action. At full pace he ran back and forth behind the mob, barking furiously and occasionally diving in to nip a heel for good measure.

Meanwhile, poor old Ho was working as hard as his arthritic joints would allow. Facing him was the whole mob, defiant and determined to escape. He blocked one then another group of breakaways, sending them back to the mob with tails high and nostrils flaring—but as he regrouped the mob on one wing, a breakaway started on the other.

Ho's exertions spurred the pup to even greater effort. The atmosphere became charged with the fear of confused bullocks being pushed around by the two dogs working in opposition.

Fred watched for a while, hoping the dogs would sort things out, but he finally decided to add to the confusion and help Ho while he shouted threats at the pup like, 'Come behind here, you bastard' or 'I'll shoot you'. He rode around the mob, cracking his whip, turning back one then another, but he knew failure was imminent. The bullocks had had enough.

Suddenly, cued by some primeval signal, the whole mob revolted. They scattered in all directions, making it impossible for dog or man to control them. Ho gave up. He knew he was defeated and let the mob go. It really wasn't their fault anyway.

As the bullocks streamed away around him, Ho ran straight for the pup who, with tongue lolling and tail wagging as he panted in the shade of a bush, was very pleased with his achievement. But the pleasure was short-lived. Old Ho wasn't at all amused.

He grabbed the pup by the scruff of the neck and shook him as he would a rabbit, at the same time scolding him for his stupidity with savage growls. The pup's yelps of fear changed to whimpers of submission. Ho dropped him but mauled some more warnings. Completely cowered, the pup rolled onto his back, baring his neck and belly, and awaited his fate.

Disgusted, Ho turned away from him, lifted his leg and peed on the bush, then trotted away to join Fred, whose laughter echoed around the ridges as they started again to muster the mob.

"Izzie hated letting me out of her sight. She had a habit of following me to work when I left her at home. She once tracked me for 30 kilometres on dirt tracks for three hours in the middle of summer to find me when I was out droving. Her appetite for work was insatiable!" Kerry Fullwood, Bulgunnia Station, south-west of Coober Pedy, South Australia.
Sally Harding, Albury, NSW

195

Lovely Linda

Emmie Cripps Northampton, WA

Years ago, in the late 1940s, we bought a pure-bred border collie pup from a breeder in Northam in WA. Her grandmother, The Horwood's Linda, was a champion sheepdog at the Royal Agricultural Show of WA and was the winner of the annual sheepdog trials on more than one occasion. Like her grandmother she was a sable colour, not the usual black and white type. Her ancestors were from Scotland.

This very intelligent wee pup arrived by train at Northampton after being some two days in transit.

We called her Linda and she learnt immediately to sit and come to us. My husband was quite surprised by her intelligence. In no time Linda could round up a small number of sheep successfully. She always stood her ground if some stubborn animal stamped its feet—Linda always won. We had always had a good sheepdog but Linda was something special, and so obedient at all times. Before long we could trust her to go out of sight and bring a small mob of sheep without leaving any behind.

We had a small sheep stud and that meant the sheep were handled more than ordinary flocks. The rams were never far from the homestead and if we wanted to check them over at any time, my husband could tell Linda to bring them to the homestead gate by pointing to where they were. While she was away he would have a quick cup of tea before walking out to see how she was coping. She would always have the sheep at the gate and would be lying down facing the mob so she could watch any sheep likely to try to escape. If they did they were soon brought back to the fold again.

When autumn came, the showery days meant the stud rams and ewes had to be shedded. There was only a small mob of ewes so they went into a small shed a short distance from the shearing shed where the rams were put. The usual procedure was to put the ewes in first, then go down the hill and bring in the rams. We would call Linda and point to the ewes and off she would go to put them into their shed. By the time we had caught up to her she would have them on their way, bound for the shed, and we just had to help them run up the ramp into the shed. She would instantly set off for the rams and, although they always protested, Linda got the upper hand and sent them to the sheepyards, up a race and into their shed. The only time she queried our orders was if the rams were closer to the shed than the ewes were. She would still want to put the ewes in first, but would reluctantly obey when we insisted.

In the north-west corner of the property we had a yard made from old branches off the trees nearby. The gate was also made from a couple of branches of jam tree. Once the sheep were inside, we pulled the branches across the gate and the sheep were secure.

One day I walked up over the hill to this makeshift yard to give my husband a phone message about a sheep sale. I waited until the sheep work had been completed, then pulled the branches back so the sheep could go out quietly. We set out for home, stopping to look at the only old quandong tree still alive on the property. I put the kettle on for morning tea and my husband had a good wash. Suddenly he looked through the flyscreen door and outside the house but he couldn't see Linda. He called her as this was unusual, but she wasn't there.

Then the penny dropped. He remembered that he hadn't told her we were finished and that she could come home with us. Although the brush gate was open, Linda had apparently remained there, guarding the sheep in the yards. When my husband arrived back at the yards, he felt so sorry for his lovely dog. He gave her a great pat and set off back home.

In time we purchased an early Land Rover with a canvas hood which was often removed. One day on the highway to Carnarvon my husband passed a large transport in a cutting six or seven miles from home. It was crawling very slowly up the hill but he quickly left it behind as he went down across the sand plain, where he met another large transport going south in a great hurry. The road was narrow so he suddenly had to pull right over onto the edge of the highway.

A few miles after this incident my husband glanced back to find, with horror, that Linda was no longer in the back. He

Maisy the freeloader. Nice work if you can get it. Darling River Floodplain, March 2007.
Jane Murray, Louth via Bourke, NSW

thought she must have overbalanced when he'd swerved to the side of the road. He turned back and stopped and whistled in the spot where he had veered sharply. There was no answer. He checked the short shrubs bordering the road to see if she was lying there unconscious.

He didn't know what to do, so he returned home and rang the police, who informed him that Linda hadn't been picked up. He added that another farmer's sheepdog had recently been stolen by a truck driver. He believed sometimes these dogs were sold to station hands for stock work.

We wondered if the transport that passed going north, which wouldn't stop, had picked up Linda. The police in Carnarvon said they would stop the truck south of the town around midnight, when the transports usually got there, and see if they had a dog that looked like her. The whole household was feeling so sad. The Carnarvon police hadn't had any luck either.

A couple of days passed and then early one morning when one of us opened the back door, there was poor Linda, looking drawn and covered in bright red mud which was caked on her long fur. She was lying down on the step. Her feet were raw from walking on stones. We had no idea how far she had travelled.

The police were pleased to hear our news and said that she must have come from near The Overlander roadhouse between Northampton and Carnarvon. It was the only area that had had a thunderstorm in the past couple of days. Otherwise she could not possibly have had a bath in a puddle, which clearly she had done. The roadhouse was nearly 100 miles away.

Linda could hardly hobble. I bathed her feet with warm water and put some ointment on them. We fed her a light diet for a few days, wrapped her up in a blanket and put a covered hot brick with her at night.

When my husband died suddenly, she mourned her loss by lying sadly at the back door. She did not live many years after that and died in her sleep. Linda—a valuable, loving animal missed by all who knew her.

Red Heeler Tizzie, keeping a watchful eye over happenings on the farm. **Joelle Wright**; photo sent in by **Lauren Fogarty, Heyfield, Vic**

Heeling instinct on hold

Les Evans Borden, WA

When I was a boy we had a little red kelpie bitch. She was the only heeler, with horses and cattle, we ever owned. On this occasion my father was doing some fence repairs along a little-used road. He had two horses standing unattended on the road hitched to a wagon. Normally they would remain like this indefinitely, but on this day a limb broke off a tree and startled them. Away they went. When Dad saw Lassie take off after them he thought, 'Oh well, that's that. I won't see the horses for a while. The wagon could break up and I'll have to walk home.'

However, instead of heeling the horses as she had always done previously, Lassie went to one horse's head and bit and barked till she had them jammed against the fence. When Dad finally got to them, Lassie was jumping up and down and her tail was thrashing happily. She had caught them and she was very pleased with herself.

It really was quite an extraordinary act since it was such a significant departure from her normal method of working. She had overruled her natural instinct to heel the horses in order to stop them.

A fine working team: Lockie, Zac and Carolynn. Zac was in his prime and unquestionably the boss, and hence got the spot closest to the driver; Lockie was the new pup on the paddocks and had to make do with a backseat hay ride; Carolynn was a uni student. Seven years on, Lockie is clearly number-one working dog; Zac retains thoughts of still being boss although, being deaf and almost blind, he is often at odds around sheep despite remaining just as keen and holding on to his preferred riding spot. Carolynn works as a nurse but she still finds time to regularly visit and undertake stock work with her two equally committed team mates. **John and Robyn Ive, Yass Valley, NSW**

Shy and white

Enid Clark Singleton, NSW

Shy was so named because she would whimper and squirm when I picked her up. She is almost completely white and has two blue eyes. I hadn't wanted a white dog but she turned out to be better than I had ever hoped. She worked for five years at Singleton saleyards in between mustering wild cattle in the mountains.

Not having wanted a white dog initially, I have found they have great advantages over red or black dogs. Cattle can see them better and can therefore be stopped more easily. In scrubby country a white dog is very easy to see in the distance and I have noticed that they don't feel the heat as much as a dark-coloured dog. Some of these factors may account for Shy's talent with cattle.

We have a small place and work casually for other graziers. On one property we mustered there were some very steep and dirty gullies and if the cattle broke we sometimes had to spend half a day getting them together again. As we approached some of these gullies, Shy would leave the mob and go ahead to wait for the breakaways. She would meet them face to face with force, rushing and jumping up and barking in their faces—which would alter 99 per cent of their minds.

Once, on another property, a breakaway heifer about eighteen months old all but knocked my husband's horse over and made for the scrub. Four dogs were sent to block it, but when we noticed that it was useless, we called them back as they were needed to take the mob to the yards a couple of miles away. Only three dogs came back and Shy wasn't one of them. We put the mob in the yard and had lunch, then went on drafting—and still Shy hadn't shown up.

After about three and a half hours we noticed a beast coming around the mountain about half a mile away, just a few feet at a time. Then, as it got closer, we could see Shy rushing in at its head. It would charge and stop. She brought it all the way into the yards. It was the wild heifer and it hadn't gotten any quieter. It had taken her approximately four hours to bring it the two miles.

Shy is ten years old now and only does the little jobs around the house. She gets the house cow and educates our weaner cattle in and out of the yards. She keeps our calves and our neighbours' calves sorted out if they get through the creek when it rains. If we truck a new house cow from our other place, and she hasn't come along to help, she makes sure the neighbours end up with it the next day. She thinks it is a stray and that it must be sent back. If she helps us bring it home, then she'll leave it here.

A couple of months ago we bought three small black calves to rear. We put them in the calf yard under Shy's supervision. Next morning, one was gone. When we let Shy off her chain, we didn't notice where she went until we heard a cow roaring and saw her coming 300–400 yards away, bringing a little black calf with the mother in hot pursuit from our neighbour's paddock. She worked the calf through the fence and brought it right to our calf pen. We didn't like to disappoint her, so we put it onto the truck to take it back to the neighbour's place.

When we arrived we were surprised to discover they had our calf tied up at their yards and were wondering who owned it. Shy must have seen ours head off into the night, so was determined to retrieve it as soon as she was free.

The troops cooling down after a hard day's work. Left to right: Bec, Molly, Cheetah and Stig.
Breanna Gregory, Pinnaroo, SA

Somewhere outside Kingaroy, in 2007, we were inspired to do a U-turn on a back road just to satisfy ourselves about what we thought we'd seen. By the time we turned back, the farmer had arrived and the dogs were ready to follow him home. However it took only a few words and indeed he called his entourage into line and ordered them back onto the fence. All fourteen dogs obeyed, as you can see. When he released them they were off like a shot and after the ute. No yelping or barking like we've come to expect of working dogs. We stood and watched, amazed, until the dust settled. **Liz and Peter Mildenhall, Bend of Islands, Vic**

Still circling

J Griffiths Beaumaris, Vic

Bob's owner was Snow Anderson, who lived in the Terrinallum district of Victoria, which suffered a devastating fire about fourteen years ago.

Bob was well known and loved. He was reaching an age when some people thought he had run his time and should be put down.

On the morning of the fire, Snow told his wife he was going to move his stock—1,600 sheep and 200 cattle—onto a bare paddock. He took Bob to help him.

While they were there, the local fire brigade came by, called Snow over and told him a big burn was rapidly coming their way. Snow was an officer in the fire brigade, so he immediately climbed up onto the truck to help fight the fire. He didn't give Bob another thought.

While Snow was away at the fire, a wind shift turned the fire over Snow's farm. His wife and children knew what to do to save the homestead and surrounds.

The firefighters worked all day, then had the heartbreaking job of shooting injured animals, and securing what was left of the properties. Late in the day, Snow returned home exhausted. His wife persuaded him to have a meal before he went out to shoot his injured stock. Snow took his gun and set off to complete the tragic day.

When he reached the paddock, Snow found his old dog, Bob, still circling the sheep and cattle. They were all safe, but Bob had burnt the pads on his paws. Snow picked him up and took him home, where the family nursed him back to health to live out the rest of his life in retirement.

The trial

Garry Somerville Mosman, NSW

This story told to me about 35 years ago is based on fact, but I have changed the names. Ben had spent all his life in the bush, mostly as a station hand, sometimes as a drover. He had wandered about central Queensland and western New South Wales, never staying long in one place.

At 75 years of age, he was a bachelor, teetotaller, non-smoker and had spent the last three years as station hand for Mr Alex Davidson on Burran Station, near Wilcannia.

A pillar of honesty who worked hard from dawn to dusk, he was an excellent sheep man who kept to himself. His sole companion was his eight-year-old red kelpie Sailor. A keen lover of dogs, Ben had acquired Sailor as a seven-week-old pup for five shillings from a passing traveller. He had taken a fancy to the pup and thought it a good 'un. His previous dog had died from distemper.

Ben was an expert with dogs, and patiently trained Sailor over the years to be an exceptionally good worker. They were inseparable and Ben never missed an opportunity to correct or encourage his charge. The results were amazing—the dog understood everything Ben said.

Sailor bedded down every night in the shearers' quarters alongside Ben, some distance from the homestead. It was common for Ben to chat away to Sailor for hours on end. They were truly great companions. Of all the dogs he had owned, Ben had an extra soft spot for Sailor, though he never let on. Wherever he went, his mate was always within scent distance.

Ben's boss considered them worth three men. When a job had to be done, these two could be relied on.

One Sunday, he remarked casually to Ben, 'The sheepdog trials are on at the showground next Saturday. Do you want me to enter you and Sailor when I'm in town today?'

Ben, no lover of crowds, hesitated for a moment, then said, 'OK, we'll give it a go.'

For the rest of the week Ben gave Sailor a good work-out with the sheep whenever the opportunity arose. Ben never stopped talking to the dog. It was as if each understood exactly the other's thoughts. The unity between them was extraordinary.

When Saturday arrived, Ben was up early and finished his chores in time to harness up the horse and trap which his boss had given him permission to use. Sailor, who usually trotted behind, was allowed up alongside Ben.

The Wilcannia showground is huge, surrounded by a picket fence, and when Ben finally arrived, the ground was crowded, with some competitors having come from as far as 50 miles away. The sheepdog trials were a popular event and everyone made an effort to be there. The entrance fee was one pound, with the winner's purse twenty-five. There were twelve entrants and Sailor had drawn No. 12.

Each competitor started with 100 points, the judge deducting points when the dog made an error. The dog and handler started from a common peg and, on a signal from the judge, the dog would be cast out by the handler to the opposite end of the ground where three sheep were standing.

The dog had to bring the sheep back to the handler as quickly as possible. It then had to take the same sheep through a drafting race and some 200 yards to a small bridge. Finally it had to drive the sheep another 200 yards, then put them in a pen. The handler then shut the gate to conclude the competition. The maximum time allowed was fifteen minutes. Points were deducted for slow work, sheep being off course, dogs overrunning and sheep breaking away from the dog.

Ben chose a cool spot on the outskirts to park the trap so Sailor could relax away from the crowd as he waited his turn. They kept to themselves, Ben just nodding occasionally to someone he knew. Most of the other competitors and spectators congregated round the start. Ben knew Sailor would need all the rest he could get if he was to put up a good show, so he was content to watch from a distance.

Promptly at 11 am, the steward blew his whistle for the first contestant. The crowd was silent. The first three dogs scored between 80 and 90 points each. The fourth dog, a huge black and tan kelpie, was very good. He made few errors and his cast was as good as Ben had seen. He got a score of 95.

Even when they appear out for the count, Eddie and Solo from 'Rosebank' in Mt Pleasant, South Australia, always have an ear to the ground listening for the boss. **Sally Harding, Albury, NSW**

'A tough one to beat,' he muttered to Sailor, who was still asleep under the trap in the shade.

The day wore on. Two other dogs scored 91 and 92, the others in the eighties.

The ninth competitor was Floss, a well-bred two-year-old border collie with good markings. A good-looking dog, Ben thought, and one he guessed would be difficult to beat.

He had heard of the collie's exploits at previous trials. Both he and his handler were well known and raised murmurs from the crowd from their bearing. The dog sat upright and willing, a good sign in trial competitions. Floss's cast and lift were neat and straight and the only fault, Ben thought, was that the young dog overran a little. A polished performer, Floss brought the three sheep straight down the middle of the ground.

At the first obstacle the collie was faultless, putting the sheep through the race perfectly with a maximum score. Ben admired this dog; he was certainly a champion. He had an air of confidence about him, and he reminded Ben of what Sailor had been like some six years ago. He looked at Sailor and smiled.

When 98 went up on the board there was a tremendous cheer. Ben realised then what they were up against. This Floss was a good one, better than any he could recall. He roused Sailor just prior to their turn.

'You'll do your best, old boy,' he whispered as he walked towards the start.

When Ben and Sailor arrived at the peg, a quietness settled on the ground in deference to their age. Sailor, with his white whiskers and muzzle, and Ben, stooped over slightly, were in direct contrast to the collie and his handler.

Sailor sat quietly at the start till the three sheep were liberated at the other end of the ground. When they were standing steady, the judge signalled the timekeeper and Ben was given the signal to start. For about ten seconds, Ben hesitated so that Sailor could get the scent. This was going to be a tough one, Ben knew.

Suddenly there was a change in Sailor. He sat upright, listening with his ear back in an antenna fashion. Ben cast him out: 'Go way back, boy!'

Sailor was off like a flash and Ben, because of the obstacles, used a shrill whistle to guide him. It was a perfect pear-shaped cast and he came up smartly behind the sheep and, on Ben's whistle, halted directly behind them.

Sailor, as if by telepathy, delivered the sheep without fault in a straight line down the centre of the field. He was precise and neat, handling them quietly but with assurance. Never for a second did he give them the opportunity to be contrary. He was indeed master of the situation, and Ben knew Sailor had gained the maximum points for his effort.

Ben's hands began to sweat. Though excited, he kept a poker face.

Ben then led the way round the fence with the three sheep behind him and Sailor taking up the rear. On reaching the drafting race, Ben stepped into the car tyre placed on the field for the handler, who has to stay there till the sheep are put through the race by the dog. Until now Sailor had not made a mistake, but just as the last sheep was about to go through the race he veered a fraction to the right. It was only for a second, but Ben knew they had lost vital points.

From the time Sailor left the starting peg, Ben had talked to him constantly, giving him encouragement and commands, and trying to keep one guess ahead of his dog.

After the race, it was 200 yards to the next obstacle, the bridge. Ben encouraged Sailor by talking to him reassuringly. Again, he could not fault his dog's effort. Once more he realised they had gained maximum points. He was at work on the sheep as soon as the last one left the bridge.

With the final obstacle, the pen, some 200 yards ahead, Ben told Sailor, 'Good boy!'

There was, unknown to Ben, whose full concentration was on his dog, a silence around the ground as everyone sensed the closeness of the scores.

'Go back, go way fore, go back.' Sailor appeared to be on a string. Everything Ben said, the dog did.

With the three sheep close by the pen and Sailor glued with his nose twitching in front of them, one paw raised as if to pounce, excitement reached its peak. Two sheep raced into the pen, with a slight movement from Sailor. One to go! Suddenly, for no apparent reason, the remaining sheep ducked out of the edge of the wing. Sailor had him back and in the pen in almost the same instant, but Ben knew as he moved to close the pen that he had lost another point.

The crowd cheered and everyone except Ben and Sailor seemed to go mad. Ben returned slowly to his trap and quietly fondled Sailor's ear. 'You went close, boy. It was a fine effort.'

When the score of 97 was marked up, a ripple again went round the crowd. Floss had won by one point. No-one had dreamed that any other dog would come near to Floss's score. However, Ben's experience told him the younger dog had deserved his win, so he tried not to let Sailor sense his disappointment.

Floss's owner, knowing how close the result had been, finally broke away from his friends and walked over to congratulate Ben on the fine performance Sailor had put up. He, too, recognised a good dog when he saw one.

He was there some minutes with Ben, and when he returned to his friends, he had a worried look and seemed at a loss for words. One of his friends joked, 'What's the matter, Alf? Anyone would think you'd lost!'

He didn't reply for some time. When he did, his voice shook. 'You saw how that old kelpie worked those sheep so close … do you know he's been totally blind for two years?'

Turbo and Dash sit quietly at smoko during a breeder muster at Boogalgopal Station, willing for some food to come their way. With eyes like these, it's hard to refuse! **Bronwyn Burnham, Eidsvold, Qld**

206

The ABC 'Wave' device is a trademark of the Australian Broadcasting Corporation and is used under licence by HarperCollinsPublishers Australia.

Top Dogs contains stories that were previously published in *Great Australian Working Dog Stories* in 2009

This illustrated edition first published in Australia in 2014 by HarperCollinsPublishers Australia Pty Limited ABN 36 009 913 517
harpercollins.com.au

HarperCollinsPublishers
Level 13, 201 Elizabeth Street, Sydney, NSW 2000, Australia
Unit D1, 63 Apollo Drive, Albany, Auckland 0632, New Zealand
A 53, Sector 57, Noida, UP, India
7785 Fulham Palace Road, London W6 8JB, United Kingdom
2 Bloor Street East, 20th floor, Toronto, Ontario M4W 1A8, Canada
195 Broadway, New York, NY 10007, USA

ISBN: 978 0 7333 3328 6

Cover and internal design by Hazel Lam, HarperCollins Design Studio
Layout by Sam Williams
Front cover photograph by Breanna Gregory
Back cover photograph by Mandy Archibald
Photographs on pages 2 and 8 by Sally Harding
Typeset in Linotype Avenir 9/12
Colour reproduction by Graphic Print Group, South Australia
Printed and bound in China by RR Donnelley on 128gsm matt art.
The papers used by HarperCollins in the manufacture of this book are a natural, recyclable product made from wood grown in sustainable plantation forests. The fibre source and manufacturing processes meet recognised international environmental standards, and carry certification.

The best times of my life were with Izzie. She got me through the worst as well. This photo was taken at Mulgathing Station, South Australia, when Izzie was eight weeks old. Izzie died last year and I miss her everyday but know she is waiting for me on the other side. **Kerry Fullwood, New Norcia, WA**

Acknowledgements

Making this book possible were the talents of many people. My thanks go to Sally Harding, an award-winning photographer and renowned snapper of dogs. Sally was instrumental in getting this book off the ground, and I am so pleased we have been able to include some of her stunning images in *Top Dogs*. I would also like to thank Tony Rasmussen and Nick Morris from ABC Local Radio for enthusiastically supporting the idea of the photo competition and turning it into a reality. I am delighted that ABC Books has embraced this project and thank them for honouring the working dogs of Australia with such an outstanding tribute. Brigitta Doyle, always positive and quick to respond to queries, her vision and drive brought this book to life. Much praise is also due to Hazel Lam and Sam Williams for the book's sparkling design and placement of photographs and stories.

Thanks, as always, to Fran Moore, my agent at Curtis Brown.

Finally, to everyone who took photographs of working dogs and sent them to be judged, very special and grateful thanks from us all. It has been a great privilege to be part of your world and to meet the dogs who are such an important part of your lives.

Angela Goode, 2014